The Fa[illegible] that Went Down to the Sea...

In Poetry

Carrol A. Buntin

Carrol A. Buntin

First Printing, November, 2005

ISBN 0-9774797-0-6
Printed in the United States of America

Published by:

Carrol A. Buntin
P.O. Box 6190
Hilo, HI 96720-8924
www.lobodelmar.com

CONTENTS

CONTENTS (Continued)

Preface

A forty-five year marriage to a man with jack-of-all trades abilities, and our offspring of seven boys and four girls has often brought us a generous-like portion of a king's table spanning from Alaska to Old Mexico and on to Hawaii with peasantry ware.

"Stretching" has been our middle name for reaching needs and desirables with an, If-we-can't-build-it, forget-it, attitude.

Rup taught our sons lay-out skills early on, and together began building our life aboard. This life we accepted as normal, on-lookers found amusing, tough and most abnormal; often suggesting we write a book, to which he replied, "You write it, we're too busy living it." (Throughout the past twenty years many newspaper and magazine articles have been written about this seafaring family.)

Later adding, "We're too busy building it." For his own catamaran design surfaced after many years of life on various monohulls.

Today, this family has encamped near the Sea of Cortez in the Sonoran Desert of Old Mexico to build live-aboard "cats" from his plans while keeping Hawaii a working base for each of the children's trades.

This fashion of life has snow-balled into uniqueness for

The Family that Went Down to the Sea...

Destiny

This man was dressed in not the best dressed clothes; but neither were they rags. His manner was polite, but reserved. Yet, he came off friendly, in a guarded kind of way. He had an air of lowly, so why did I curtsy within? His speech was drawled a bit, but plain and down to earth. I got the strangest feeling that he could talk to almost anyone about almost any subject. His eyes were questioning, but I caught myself fumbling with the lattice of my heart to keep them out. A glimmer flashed to his eyes, but melted away respectfully. Thank you for the extended scepter, I thought, and my privacy. I met this man, again, another day. He was the same. But as we talked I felt the shield slowly fall. I saw a boy, lonely, with an innocence I can't explain for a man his age. Few words were needed, or even desired. When we parted, I couldn't believe how close I'd felt to him. When we met again there was an urgency! I'd wanted to make small-talk and enjoy the moment, but a warning stronger than joy prevailed. If I didn't heed, I'd lose this once-in-a-lifetime man. My heart stopped! A wave of fear swept over me. The next day I married this man destined for me. I am at peace. I am in love with a king's son.

Time, Always

If our tomorrow never comes, would you go with me today?
By giving up your flare of fun would you settle for my ways?
Could you leave your home, sufficient, to live insufficiently?
Should you be so kind for staying if hard luck hit heavily?
Cause I'd make your day forever; what's tomorrow left to God.
As I've spent a lifetime dreaming, but without you, plans would stop.
Though I haven't much to offer but with you, we'd have an edge.
So if hard times come, whatever, you by my side, I would pledge.
Would a pauper ask one blinded 'follow him to outer star
and expect no questions asked him but to tag along that far?
That's how out-of-reach this match seems. I'm without an answer, one.
But a love that needs no reason is the reason ours has come.
Come and share the ocean wonders and explore the Seven Seas.
Ride the four winds way up yonder, and the slip stream, if you please.
I'll not need you more than always, so let always be our vow.
Be prepared for me to please you, for our time to live is now!

In the Sixties there was a fireman on the City of Las Vegas Fire Department getting a little carried away in thought while trying to make ends meet for his family as an engineer/fireman in town, and fire chief of a village where he lived.

This Blue Diamond, fifteen miles from Vegas, was a company town of Flintcote Corporation, ideal home site for them. And true to form, the fire that was being built in him was one that COULD be put out with WATER.

Rupert, Sr. and Rupert, Jr., Texas

Rett and Ruppy on First Boat, San Leandro, CA, Marina.
Even the old Budha Engine was still in "Cosmolene" from World War II.

The Beginning

When at last it reached the station taking hold the men and squad,
Well he knew, the trends approaching would force him to leave his job.
Vegas was his home since Sixty, that he'd grown to love sincere.
In the Hills he was the Fire Chief, in the City, Engineer.
"Doesn't leave us much to cling to," weren't the words to her surprise.
"Guess I'll move us on a boat," were. Stunned, but she made no reply.
Oftentimes the change of subject got her man on other schemes.
Not this time; the nightmare came true. Soon she too was chasing dreams.
With their sons she combed the harbors searching all the ports in vain.
But the quote that raised her hackles was, "Now, lady, you're insane!"
That gave her determination. Time to prove there's more to life.
Can't stuff some folks in a bottle. Nau-ti-cal became her life.
Tucked away and still in moth balls, was a launch meant just for them;
needing paint and restoration, just like them, to live again.
All the hidden fears she'd harbored for her children from day, one,
left the moment they all boarded their new boat, new life, new home.

The sea is a reflection of nature. Its Spartan life that took us into its fold had started filling our vessel with after-the-fact tales long before this little mermaid surfaced.

In the beginning few months of Rup's four year stint in the Navy he stayed seasick, and green, continually looking back towards land.

But on a Destroyer Escort, in one of its worst storms, maneuvering its typical under-two-waves and over-one, he recovered from those blahs never to look back again.

Rup in the Navy, 1950,
San Diego, California

Destroyer Escort,
Rup's ship in the Navy

Anchors Aweigh in Nature

In nature there's a flood that sweeps in from sea's grip to shore,
and then the tide leaves out again to chase the waves once more.
This carefree life of back and forth while day and night times play,
makes reeling to and fro at sea the sailor's trademark, sway.
The trade winds treading out each course bid passing doldrums, "Bye."
A Spartan's life foretold for all as land-free sea life try.
Found swabbing up the sea front floor while swapping yarns and fibs,
that shore's so nice to visit, Mate, just no place fit to live!
The slapping on the starboard hull by winds, tides, waves in turn;
just nature's way to pipe aboard, "Anchor's aweigh, affirmed!"

Herbert Fujimoto came into our lives in Alviso, California soon after we boarded our new home. He worked for Peterbuilt, and spent his weekends with us. The cabin door would swing open and the biggest box of Winchell's Donuts would walk in, with Fuji trailing behind grinning, and kicking off his shoes.

During the day he'd head topside to watch transformation of the boat and aggravate the kids.

In the meanwhile, Rup and the boys had spent a week hand-drilling Holes in stainless steel pipes for substantions.

It was Fuji's concern and care for "his" kids that forced him to spend a sleepless night doing some awesome knot-tying to make a net suitable for a life line.

The morning he and I stood on the dock waving farewell to Rup and the boys, before my departure also, would be a scene branded deep with emotions because of an adoption that had truly taken place.

Fuji had lost his girlfriend during the Pearl Harbor attack in December 1941.

USS Nevada
War Memorial

Uncle Fuji and Brady,
Pleasant Harbor, Washington

Uncle Fuji's Starlite Sailboat
Carson, Washington

Uncle Fuji

There's a page of the Log that is missing from the Isle
that we trace in the journals of our heart.
Brings to mind, one man's life who felt best friends were but few,
and with us, shared a friendship from the start.
Years ago, on the morn that the "Islands" paid a price, he paid,
too; lost his sweetheart, his first love.
Yes, his heart went with her, for he never took a wife.
Loved his friends like an angel from above.
We moved on our new boat in Alviso, near the "Slew",
where we met and adopted our new friend.
As we built to our home, he in turn built on it, too.
There was room for our Uncle to the end.
Once he left, while still day, to tie knots all through the night,
making sure his kids' safety, first was kept.
While we laced his tied net to the life line on the deck,
he could dream, knew he couldn't, had he slept.
On the banks of the "Slew" he was there to bid farewell,
and his thoughts of our voyage never dimmed.
But he, too, sailed one day, to an Isle, not far away;
here's Your page of Ole Fuji, our best friend!

When the tide was out in Alviso Slew, boats sat on a mud bottom. This mud had endurance.

Chres, a friend, had made the Pacific crossing in a trimaran with that mud stuck fast-to the bottom, and after his return voyage verified it still remained part of the keel.

Rup worked in the busy city of San Jose as a welder for F.M.C. But our slip-space was situated on an ideal spot between all the major cities of the Bay.

Obviously, we weren't the only lucky dogs to stumble upon this oasis.

Alviso, California — Destination of our maiden voyage from San Leandro, California

Alviso Slew

No one ever 'planned' a party living in the "Slew."
Most the boarders had, "to do" lists chalked up for their crew.
Boat repair and reconstruction were the basic aim.
Walks of life were represented. No one had the same.
In Alviso camped a "Hippy;" cross the bay, a jerk.
Chres, next stall, lived on his sailboat. Lockheed's where he worked.
Mike, the Greek, and daring Bobbie—not a couple, though,
both had their respect for boat life; both would tell you so!
Sundays always brought the 'lookers' peering in at us.
Made us all feel just like "monkeys", making such a fuss!
We lived like "Old hidden treasures" near the cities' hubs.
Compassed all about, but hidden, free from their hub-bub.
Maybe one might come to borrow, or return a trawl;
didn't matter, always unplanned, party time for all!

When Rup headed out with the three oldest boys Ruppy, Rett, and Brent under the Golden Gate to make their way up the rugged coasts of California and Oregon to Washington, we estimated the trip to take two or three weeks.

February was not the wisest of months to be out testing boat structure, but need seemed greater than caution, and that being employment.

It would be a seemingly endless journey of weather watching and harbor-hopping. The seas permanent attitude made Rup "religious" about not sticking his nose out without a long-range forecast. Even with it, many times, the weather failed to obey.

Rup's friend, Dewey, and his son of 21 started the trip two weeks after. Before hand, Rup had me call him with warnings and advising against it. But he said he was a "Big Boy." The Coast Guard gave up search for them many years ago.

Three long months later, Rup and his crew tied up at Cascade Locks, Oregon, needing much repair—boat and braves. A hop and a skip across the Columbia River would soon after be our new home on Wind River. In Washington, Ruppy, along with his brothers, had turned into top-notch seamen...FIRST CLASS!

Ruppy and wife, Sue today

Ruppy Storms

Storms at sea so unforgiving, when mistakes by man are made.
"Do exactly as I tell you," warned his father as he bade:
"Jump, when I say jump, don't tarry!"
Second-thought could mean their doom.
Raging waters have no mercy. For an error, there is no room.
Eldest of the seven boys; never harmed when taking heed.
If his brothers failed to follow, he was there to take the lead.
On their maiden trip from 'Frisco,' underneath that Golden Gate,
hind-sight tells them, now, the reason for charts sold-out 'round the Cape.
Mom and babe with girls to help her, left by car up North, that morn.
Unaware that Mendocino held her men-folk in a storm.
With the pounding boat, dad steered them out to sea—their only hope.
Through the darkness, by a compass, Ruppy watched as dad's own scope.
With the morning light came calmness. Each one knew who'd had control.
Tossed and torn, a tad bit wiser; wonders of the deep unfold.
Dad has quite a crew of sailors, and he's proud of everyone.
But in storms, if asked his first choice, it would be his eldest son.

We've had millionaire friends and we've had hippy friends. Two different paths, with ours making three, and our only common ground is that we all enjoy God's creation.

It's not necessary that we accept one another's philosophy and belief, but we should and can help each other.

The Bottom Line

We've spent so many twilight hours with friends expressing dreams;
the choice to live on sea puts us at risk, to them, it seems.
The sea still roars out in the deep, and yes, we still must trust;
but each has had a problem understanding this of us.
I fret not if they don't believe in whom I pledge my vows,
for I, in turn, allow them slack to honor whom, and how.
The bottom line is not how much that men should be the same,
but if they'll live that rule of gold with turn-about fair game.
For who's to say what beat is heard in yet another's heart?
The drummer's roll may strike a rhythm from a different chart.
Would be a waste to worry how each man abides his time,
and goad interpretation on the dictates of his mind.
Commitment warns me follow paths where my allegiance lay;
watch that I tread life cautiously so they don't curse my faith.

Still thankful that a future place for us to occupy would be special, though unforeseen by us.

The first years of married life, we tried to be as solid a citizen as the next, I suppose; but still there seemed to be something missing.

Renting a new place, while following Rup's trade would often be fruitless the first few days, because of our large family. But my little prayer of "a foot in the door," the "book, instead of the cover, read," was always answered because the "proof's in the puddin!"

My Solitaire

Solitaire, but not confined,
belongs to men who choose the seas.
Hardships they have felt on waves
as lifelines drift outstretched to seize.
Dauntless Captains aren't dismayed
but often fearful midst a storm.
Intuition guides their judgments
and the ships on which they're borne.
Skippers come a dime-a-dozen,
masters, still, with crafts they run.
"Three cheers!" for each Commodore
and "Bravo!" for all jobs well done!
Greatest men the whole world over
find their place on sea and ship—
stout and burly, strong of body,
all at one time's crossed our lips.
In my heart the unknown hero,
hid from most, but loved by me,
is the man who taught his family
how to love and claim the sea.
Sagas weren't his tools of teaching
but a hand-in-hand affair,
as he led us to the water,
we each found that God was there.

The navigational pull that attracts daydreamers and dream makers alike, lets us cross paths frequently.

When there's to be any leaving, we've never liked the left-behind feeling, and have preferred the "walking" to the "talking."

John, a hippy friend near the Olympic National Forest in Washington, was the one with the sound advice about "Big Macs." I think he meant, **K**eep **I**t **S**imple, **S**tupid.

Decision

Seems like mankind spends their life in hopes to live the way we do,
saving for the day that they'll be free to make that dream come true.
It's so hard to understand that if they put the price too high,
they'll be always chasing rainbows or their pie up in the sky.
Does the price compel them chase it, or the fact that it's a dream?
Better make a wise decision, three-score, ten years aren't extreme.
If we're each allowed one go 'round, and the facts are pretty clear,
how come all the fuss in waiting when that bucket's one-step nearer?
Make a list and check the balance, with your price can you afford
to put off your day of freedom for a few more days to horde?
And your dreams, have they prepared you
for your jump-off day that's here,
but, in fact, are they just daydreams that you tease because of fear?
Sacrifices are a blessing traded off for peace of mind.
You can only hold one Big Mac and one milkshake at a time.

Because of the many peaceful moments on the sea, there has always been a time to recollect, to be alone.

Rup was an only child, as he had lost his little sister (whom he named) in infancy. Loosening his grip from her would cause him to cling a little tighter to his future family.

Rup, his Mom and Dad looking out at sea.
Pleasant Harbor, Olympic Peninsula, Washington

Peggy Joe/Little Sis

I wonder what she'll think of me; my walk across this land?
Will she be proud, like I of her, when I last held her hand?
That Navy hitch, the culprit which enticed me from the start,
and never let me drift too far, kept tugging at my heart.
The way of life for land-locked men brought me no peace of mind.
When that door swung ajar, I rushed back closer to my kind.
I felt compelled to take the path which led down to the sea,
with wife in hand, and children, too, to raise my family.
So often, I was blind, yet Someone else was eyes for me.
As there's no greater test than when you're tried upon the sea.
But looking back within the eyes of each our grown kids, now,
I feel the charts mapped-out attest a special course, somehow.
At any given time I'd stopped the world to had her board.
But hope, indeed, when my time comes, with my sweet Sis, I've scored.

Rup, Ruppy, Rett, Brent, Bart, Brady, Brandy & Buck, Pavy & Chapo...Grandkids

Rup had always encouraged the boys to look toward adult-hood instead of playing their lives away.

It's inevitable that manhood does show up, and the voice of experience says preparation makes it a lot easier to face with a little "know-how" built in.

He tried to have them well on their way to a trade before teenagers.

Six of our sons...Bucky's absent

If they have ever backed-ears about some boyhood training, it was never this one. They began very young being proud to stand toe-to-toe with college boys.

A funny story about a college guy in Pleasant Harbor digging ditches alongside Ruppy, 14 and Rett, 13. His quote: "See, it pays to have a college education!"

Rup and six of our sons in Texas...Brent was in Mexico

Do or Die, Boys

Raised on the edge, his seven sons
had just one path to follow;
though "chin-up, straight ahead," for them
was sometimes hard to swallow.
Dad always worked at work like he
was fighting snakes at full-speed,
so every chore his young bucks did
was 'do or die,' since puppies.
To pamper, took up space so moods
were soothed as things got cracking;
the golden rule out on the edge:
there's little room for slacking.
"and be an island," dad advised,
"leave room enough for laughter,"
with trust his work and words suffice—
his rough necks follow after.
Survival was his reason—don't
shirk work with manhood nearing.
Seat-of-the-pants, by all accounts,
a lad's best way of rearing.

As the season departure from one port of call to the next nears, this entire crew gets anxious and eager. Never has it been a hang-up not to be able to pick-up and leave at a given time, or not given.

Never lived anywhere where we couldn't find something to like about the place, and at the same time no place has ever quite fulfilled the private utopia of each.

We go, we stay, we rat-hole memories.

Carson, Washington

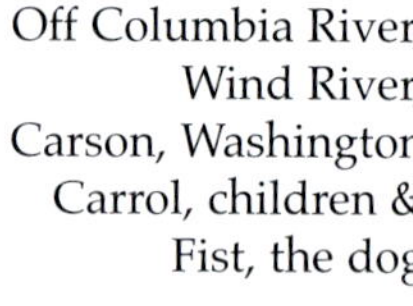

Off Columbia River, Wind River, Carson, Washington Carrol, children & Fist, the dog

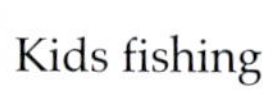

Kids fishing

Yesteryears

The "Lower Forty-Eight," from where the 'good life' for us sprung,
had gifts of sorted nature we unwrapped,
and Washington, the State, like mother eagle with its young
would prod us near the brink so we'd adapt.
Have you forgotten, son, our old Wind River's home back there—
while tied up to a log boom near its banks?
The 'Frisco passage, prior, had left our boat in great despair
but not a sweeter place to mend the planks.
The bitter weeks to follow, like a domino effect—
your dad's bad fall at work began the twist;
then, next, your older brother's decommissioned hand on deck,
about the time that ivy got your sis.
This left two sets of shoulders just the size of you and me
to carry out the details for each day.
We made that crate of lemons dealt, taste lemonade-ish, squeezed
and used the future tense like kids at play:
"With toes up in the feathers, reading comic books for fun,
we'll look back on these hardships thrown our way.
But time will be on our side, hard-to-swallow woes gone, son,
We'll sip our tea and recall yesterday."

Brena was nicked-named "Little Bit" by her great grandmother, and she was! Today, she's taller, but inside a giant. She may be the youngest girl and the eighth child but that hasn't kept her at the back of the class.

Because she's a math-wiz, her career began at the Bank's loan department and always tending the family's books. I for one wouldn't argue with her pencil.

She's now an electrician working alongside her brothers and brother-in-law.

Her disposition is the fun part—quiet, harmless, but like her dad, a roller coaster within.

Don't push her buttons—or her Buntins!

Brena/Bully

Youngest sis and dad, one day,
were watching people pass
intently staring, while she tugged
at him and softly asked,
"Do you see that little girl?"
as dad looked to respond
and saw the pretty little lass
with soft curls, long and blond.
He sweetly told his darling child,
"Of course, and she's a doll,"
completely unaware his girl
had bad intent, at all.
But just as softly, once again,
she spoke, though more abrupt,
quite assured she set her jaw,
"I can beat her up!"

One of the best pieces of advice I've heard is, "It's the next step you take."

Not only is it a challenge but also another chance to get it right.

When Rup told this to our youngsters (more than I could count) it would pick me up, too.

Brandy, Brady and Buck —
Card Sharks
Ketchikan, Alaska

Dealt By God

Down through life there've been a lot of helpless 'losers' caught betwixt,
who could only play the hand, which God had dealt.
While the clouds of misery hovered, some desired to call it quits;
others played their cards in spite of how they felt.
Had these ever turned away or folded from this match of life,
even with the battle's overwhelming odds;
they'd have lost their ante quickly, instantly souls would have died,
leaving winnings turned back over, then, to God.
Status symbol for the upper class is always judged by wealth,
so it's quick to label failure's cause as 'sin;'
not the least prepared when tables start to turn upon itself,
cursing as the 'losers' triumph in the end.
Even with a Full-house showing, Flush of King or Queen made known:
high-card holders fail where titles matter not.
For a house can lose its status quo, a Royal pair, dethroned;
door prize goes to ones who play the cards they got.
We've not all been blessed with genius, and mistakes have not been few.
What's an 'under-dog' to do, for goodness sakes?
Well, the winning hand is known already, 'losers' will not lose,
if remembered, it's the next step that we take!

Bunny is our second daughter and number five in the line-up. She was "holding and lining up" boards and nails for her dad from the very first purchased fish boat's conversion. Interest in flying took off, so George, a family friend and ex-helicopter pilot in Alaska took her "under his wings" teaching his own version of ground-school to her. Next, sending her for the official test, but with her score of 94, he laughed! (He was fully prepared to cushion her disappointment of failure by informing her that it took him more than once to pass it!)

Bunny, 1st Grade
Carson, Washington

Bunny and Rupert building Ruppy's
First boat, Pleasant Harbor, WA
"Get that nail in there, man!"

When she was young, the Columbia River Gorge was her playground, so was there that the Wind River, and its banks, became her "stepping stone."

Bunny, today,
Hawaii

Honey Bun

On the banks along the river
little girls were hard at play.
Nearby, watching, was their sister
to protect them should they stray.
From her youth she'd had compassion
for each sibling all the same,
always been a little pillar
holding-up the family's name.
Throughout life the chain she'd run from
was the 'rut' that binds and chokes;
for she'd loved the freedom taught her,
as a small lass, by her folks.
Just because she'd listened to them
when they guided her from wrong,
there's a melody within her
she can claim for her own song.
Yes, her father's love for airplanes
put the same love in her heart.
As she tips the wings up yonder,
she'd been proud she made the start.
Where her destiny will lead to
is dictated by some One,
but one thing we know she will Bee
is our sweetest HONEY BUN!

Our move from the Gorge in Washington was by truck this time. We had the boat transported from Washugal to Olympia and launched into the Puget Sound...THE VITAMIN B!

No moorage available in Seattle, led us to the beautiful and quiet, Pleasant Harbor on the Peninsula and then later to Port Townsend where we would add fifteen feet to the SEA WOLF. (Future boat, another story.)

This move in the meantime had begun a lasting friendship for us with Jann and her daughter, Barbara. Jann had followed in the footsteps of her mother and aunts as a registered nurse. In fact, her mother, Rhoda France, was Director of Nurses in Bremerton, Washington (BIG CHIEF, you might say!)

Later, her new husband would become a friend, too.

Bob, Jann & Barbara
Silverdale, Washington

Jann/Bob

It shouldn't sound outrageous, now, to move a live-aboard
across dry land two hundred miles, that came out from the Gorge.
Still at the time, those haulers claimed they hadn't moved our size,
in fact, this type, the first to be transported in their lives.
We made this move to Puget Sound where aide for health was near
and met the gal who soon became our best friend through the years.
She lived secluded in the hills to raise her little child,
an R.N., but an injury had doomed her nursing style.
My husband had been injured from a fall that placed him there,
where she, in turn, was getting help to cope through rehab care.
We helped her find a boat and moved them on when it arrived.
They moored near Hood Canal where she began to come alive.
"There's someone out there just for you, when faithful you remain,"
my husband said to her as they shared kindred thoughts and pain.
One day the SEA W0LF headed north and left our good friend, blue.
Along come Bob and married Jann, now he's our dear friend, too.

Babette, our first born, is an Idahoan far, far from home. The greater part of her life has been lived everywhere, practically, but there.

B.B. soaked up "know-how" like a sponge from early on, and now, as an adult remains just as inquisitive as her father.

And when she married, did they sail off into the sunset? On the contrary, as they took our first boat, THE VITAMIN B, moored where we moored and tagged along the Inside Passage with us to Alaska. Along for the ride was our first grandchild, Rachael Leah.

Babette and Husband, Lars

Rachael Leah and BB

Bo, Trevor, Joe, Rachael and Gretchen (Lars and Babette's children)

B.B/School Ends—Life Begins

"Do I have to finish school?" she quietly placed each word.
According to my family's roots, her question was absurd!
The best course taken here for me was to her dad be sent.
Oh, sure I followed close behind to watch him rave and "rent!"
To my surprise, he questioned her on why she felt this way;
as I kept thinking to myself, "You'll graduate in May!"
She lay her heart out on the line. He reasoned back. I moaned!
Their conversation settled; she would work around her own.
For she had yearned to learn more of the life at sea we'd known;
environment and marine life, that were all a part of home.
A shell-fish job come opened in some college student's field,
but "Beebs" won out with her and soon was trained in lab-work skills.
She met her future husband there; he'd had some college years.
Biology, Marine in fact, was one of his careers.
The best part is the next to come: they wed and took a boat;
began their dream, as we should have, two seafarers' lives afloat.

This small town of Brinnon, with Quilcene a few miles further on Washington's Peninsula would begin the wrap-up of public schools for our children in the very near future.

When school was over each evening, our kids would be dropped off at the top of the hill near the Harbor. As soon as the bus was out of sight, the boys "let down their chests." They always had lots of fun ribbing each other about this nightly incidence.

The oldest two boys would TRY to march the smaller ones down the hill in single file. We'd catch this sight from our boat, occasionally, and be quite entertained. However, there was always an out-of-step rebel. This would be Brent!

Pleasant Harbor, Brinnon, Washington

Pleasant Harbor/Children on Board

Our stay in Pleasant Harbor was precisely that for us.
Close by, there was a three-room school our six could reach by bus.
The elder two attended school a few more miles away.
Then that left us with two small tykes who had no qualms to play.
Our family's size had always raised a topic for debate,
so moving to a new place no bands played to congregate.
But after we were there awhile folks learned, a bit surprised,
that we with, almost, all our wit were, somewhat, humanized!
My husband's fall had left us counting pennies many times.
"How did the families cope on land?" a thought that crossed our minds.
Our peace of mind dwelt on our boat when vision seemed obscured.
We'd given thanks that it was bought before his fate occurred.
We caught ourselves comparing life on land to this on sea.
The nightmares that each move entailed, still frightens even me.
But when we had to re-locate this home so many times,
'bout all the effort that involved was just cast off the lines.

Bridget is the third of our girls and child, seven. As her name, she is probably the most Irish of the clan—curly hair, green eyes and wit.

Bridget & me, 1970 in Rupert, Idaho

This attitude provoked by Rup when she was six, in the poem (supposedly) is still her make-up at twenty-seven.

Bridget's talented with a carpenter's hammer and has an eye for design, so has completed the interior of two catamarans from styrofoam and paneling to cushions and carpets.

No matter the tasks of her dad's; if around she's right there with him to lend a helping hand.

Bridget and Brenda, Mexico, today

Bridget and husband, Ben, Hawaii

Bridget/Tender

We've four girls, who, when they tried,
could be so lady-like,
and so, their dad would tease them some
to check their "other" side.
Outside, as he was chasing off
the neighbor's cat again,
he saw our second youngest gal
at play, but watching him.
He made believe he'd choke the cat
while laughing up his sleeve,
and sure enough, she ran inside,
so thought she'd gotten peeved.
Instead, she summoned all the kids
to come on out, the brat!
She told them all to gather 'round,
"Dad's gonna choke the cat!"

The good news for today—NO SCHOOL! Port Townsend, along the Peninsula and the Hood Canal, wouldn't be just a haven for boat lovers and fishermen but would also bring education to migrants from a different book.

Dr. Fudala, the woman in charge, would be responsible for bringing about this program and grant not only for families on boats but any others with the same need in education.

It was on her door, after many fruitless months of denial, that Jann and I had finally knocked and very gratefully witnessed this Grant put on the table.

Hood Canal, Washington

Bunny, Brandy, Brena, Buck, Brent, Bridget, Bart, & Brady

School Fund

Whether we could pick them up, that day, from off the beach;
weather, was the factor that had kept them out of reach.
We had left the harbor to move closer to our "Doc,"
changing schools, the meanwhile, put our children in a spot.
Winter hit unusual with a heavy, early snow;
caught off-guard, the school kids stranded, with no place to go.
Quickly as this crisis ended, to each school we went,
asking for assignments fitting for this freak event.
"Can't be put together," was the absent-minded quote.
Teachers from each school reluctant; 'fraid to rock the boat.
But Port Townsend had the answer. One could solve it all.
Education for all migrants would begin that Fall.
Fifty students were computed, needing help like ours,
but the fund lay undetected, till she used her powers.
Programs like this bring a blessing, aides to teach our own.
Correspondence would come foremost, in our future home.

La Push, Washington

The sea is rough, and so, too, its pupils. It teaches hard lessons and doesn't always give credits in the course of seamanship.

Schooner Rig, Port Townsend, Washington

Mile, Two

On the ocean vision clears some, far away from man-made smog.
Obscured only to use caution when rolled in by nature's fog.
Time to size-up where we're headed and if goals are still the same.
Hindsight's always twenty/twenty, used to often check our aim.
Nonconformist? In a pig's eye! Patriotic to the core.
Paid each due to God and Country, now the fight's a different war.
Not strategic games and warfare, as giant missiles launched at sea,
but morality's own freedom maimed by bent democracy.
Question not mob's strength on their terms.
Best to cradle thoughts you own.
Don't sell-out for any reason! Wisdom comes through battles known.
If one has to drift to seaward just to keep his morals pure;
there's no price to put on self-worth. Loneliness, man can endure.
So, he wants to live a sailor, or to try the gypsy's style,
makes no difference what path taken, if he'll go that second mile.

The SEA WOLF was our second boat and had been built in the Seventies by an older man, Glenn, near Seattle.

Port Townsend, Washington, boat yard & the SEA WOLF with the first 2 holes cut in the stern.

Just like building a roof!

We met this German man and his boat in Pleasant Harbor. He fell off of it in a storm one night. Rup and the boys rescued him (our dog's barking should have first mention, here) and he lost his courage to continue living on board. Glenn made us a deal we couldn't refuse, later, so much later we would be adding fifteen foot to it and lots of fuel tanks.

The 15' has been added!

In the meantime, Hood Canal had become, from countless experiences, an excellent adventure and good home. For when its bridge to the peninsula blew down in a storm and left many without electricity and quite rattled, we stayed afloat with good T.V. and tucked in for a good night's sleep.

The finished work of art, 3 weeks later: THE SEA WOLF

BUT then there's the flip-side to the coin — the cruise!

Five Generations:
Rachel (granddaughter),
B.B. (daughter), Rup,
Granny (Rup's Mom),
Little Mama (Rup's grandmother),
on the SEA WOLF at
Hadlock, Washington
in the Hood Canal.

The Cruise

Some friends had tagged along with us to cruise up Hood Canal,
along the way, the cable to the steering went afoul.
Of course, the weather for the day from radio reports
was good, with not a chance of squall, or gale, or storm of sorts.
As soon as we had passed into the Narrows 'round the Spit,
a storm arose, and we took on some waves I'd not forget.
Without the helm, Rup rushed astern and didn't miss a beat,
the quadrant in the bilge became the steering for his feet.
While watching aft, he'd steer the boat to keep the right approach
and knew if one wave caught him wrong, the boat was sure to broach.
The sea was so tumultuous, as I checked each child for fright,
as all the members of this cruise had turned from green to white.
Up in a bunk, I checked my child, her eyes were both closed tight.
"I want to be asleep," she said, "when my time comes to die."
The memories of this trip are some we'll always keep alive.
Things funny now, but not so then, we're thankful we'd arrived.

Brent Boat-Building, Gorman, Texas

Brent is number three son, fourth child of our family and has managed to whittle out a trade in carpentry that's quite awesome. This trade has been a dynamic contribution to the family.

One night in Mexico, he and his dad were teasing about the type of poem that could possibly ever be written about such a wandering soul as he—this wild child.

He had sowed oats in the past that weren't digestible, but he was home now. We're very, very proud of his turn around.

Brent, relaxed, today

Anyway, so I could be included in their joke, I tossed this silly poem at him. He would never let me get rid of it.

Interior of 57′ boat

Brent/Boats

Once upon a time
there was a little boat.
It was very small
and it would hardly float.
Once there was a boy
and he just hated school.
While the others worked hard,
he broke every rule!
If his teacher said to
write his A-B-C's,
he'd draw only boats
that sail the Seven Seas.
About some special poem,
each kid would try to quote,
but this was all he said,
"Once there was a boat."
If by chance you peek
within his folder, now,
instead of tests you'd find
him drawn upon the bow.
Asked to speak his mind
he'd blush and start to mutter,
"If we're to live on land
how come all this water?"
This boy is now a man,
carefree as can be!
Bet you would never guess
he's building boats for free!

Man loves his boat! It's his pet. He takes control at the helm—a midget in proportion to the ship it steers. I'd wager dogs and boats were created before women. Rup named his boats. I named his kids. He snaps to attention when some seadog bellows his boat logo in salutation.

But stumbles down the roll-call of his children to give an order. By the time he hits the bottom (unsuccessfully) one of them is kind enough to answer anyway.

SEA WOLF
Thomas Basin, Alaska

Ward Cove Marina, Ketchikan, Alaska

Distinction Named

Living in and 'round the harbors names of folks may not compute.
Vivid, though, and quick to recall, names on boats that they commute.
'dollar for the times we've answered to the logo of our boat.
Owners of a yacht, we'd then be, but still nameless on the float.
Wisely picked are names we cherished; made each christened craft feel new.
Valued, but not half distinctive, names we chose for all our brood.
Often asked why choice of "B" names chanced to be the favored pet.
Answer comes most matter 'factly, "Second in the alphabet!"
Growing up along the sea ports, kids may fail their Math and Lit
knowledge asked, yet, on some vessel, not much chance that they'll forget.
So, what's in a name holds weight here, just as tonnage rules the waves,
that the ensign on each nameplate is renown in sea front ways.

A lot of water under the bridge since coming across the Columbia Bar with Astoria, Oregon on one side of it and Ilwaco, Washington on the other.

SEA WOLF somewhere near Friday Harbor, Washington

SEA WOLF in inland waters of Canada—porpoises lead the way to Alaska.

Shrimping would become an exciting part of our daily detail and an enjoyable task of employment in the Hood Canal. But I'm forced to believe that "contentment" plagues the 'old man' after a time.

So, after sweeping ashes from the decks that Mount St. Helens had left when she blew her stack a few weeks earlier, we set sail; four boats, family and friends.

Toward Northern Lights!

North to Alaska

The SEA WOLF with three other boats was anchored late one day
somewhere along the passage of the Inland Water Way.
We'd crossed the wild Queen Charlotte Sound some days before in fear
and felt the pow'r of open sea 'gainst boat, the crew and gear.
But peaceful silence in this cove where eagles chose to stay,
was broken only by the !splash! of otters prone to play.
One day we left Port Townsend Bay, as friends waved from the shore,
not half prepared for all the sights that nature had in store.
The boys would dive for Dungeness — our supper, a la crab,
while all three families climbed aboard our boat to eat and gab.
We passed through verdant forests always luscious and serene,
and trod the endless beaches, wild, secluded and pristine.
At last we reached the Dixon to Alaska's wild frontier,
and knew our trek toward NORTHERN LIGHTS would be a trip endeared!

Mt. McKinley, South to Valdez, Alaska

This man standing on the fan-tail of his world surveying all that he belongs to and all that belongs to him is the epitome of every grain of salt Rup is made of.

Home on the Brine

Across the Pole the North Wind blows a breath of frigid spray;
this artic breeze rolls to the sea and ice-caps wind and wave.
A shiver down his spine has nudged a sailor back inside;
while topside rail and deck attempt to brace against the night.
Though anchorage in these waters, northward, pleased until the frost,
at season's change one wagers with his life that could be lost.
Each porthole, dogged securely, offers momentary cheer;
yet fails to hide the ocean outside, cold with winter near.
How quickly "elsewhere's" summoned—trading places in his mind;
the answer for survival for a life lived on the line.
Warm weather, white-washed beaches on some distant sunny isle
are mind-games he'd concocted just to cope a little while.
No anguish, mixed with drear, will stow the boat away to freeze,
if warnings of the storm he'll heed of sailing safer seas.
With compass pointed South and anchor swinging free from fault,
this hard-tack knows no boundaries — home is anywhere there's salt.

When we left Ports along the way with folks enquiring about our planned destination or whereabouts, Rup would often say, “Don’t know. When we go through that break-water we’ll turn to port or to starboard. We’ll know when we get there.”

Hilo, Hawaii — a very nice little town and very similar to Port Townsend, WA

The Master Helmsman

Their life, that only God could judge, has been like ocean tide;
it often gave, then took away—for this, the Helmsman cried.
Old habits that were hard to shake and careless thoughts acquired,
proved cargo for them, hazardous—of these the Helmsman tired!
They'd left so many ports behind not knowing what to do.
But sometimes, somehow, prayer was heard—the Helmsman heard it, too.
Their faith would shake from stem to stern when deep blue sea was grieved.
But soon compassion's breath was felt—because the Helmsman breathed.
They'd have long ago jumped ship if their chains had been unlocked.
Much wiser to abide on board—until the Helmsman docked.
Their passion for the sea returned as each storm lost its thrill,
and fear had lost its challenge with the Helmsman at the wheel.
Their documented vessel, soon, will loose each burden hauled.
The plotted course will lead them to the Helmsman's Port of Call.

The flow of life on board with its happenings, no matter how trivial, centered around the cook, doctor, nurse maid and first mate...me.

Promoting "me" to new positions, temporarily until their desired goal was achieved, was common.

In a nut shell, this family revolves around the first aid kit, the galley, coffee pot and "mom."

Carrol on Thomas Basin dock, Alaska

"Mom" and Dutch, today

Your Kingpin, Queen

Full, won't scratch the surface of the type of life we've shared.
Recollect the past with me, again.
Milestones marked on land and sea as two became a pair,
still belief escapes us now and then.
Count the miles across the Country with each new job found.
Following your trade kept life afresh.
All the knots on sea, each move; each trip, can't start to count.
Navigating, we can only guess.
In our darkest moments when the outside closed its door,
closer than the problems we became.
Magnetism ruled! We felt attraction even more.
Glad, "repel" has never been our game.
Coffee break, that social hour, a vise we both share blame.
Always seemed to keep the wolves at bay.
Plans and dreams and "what to do?" with some child raising "Cain,"
solved with every pot we brewed that day.
Built around the "kingpin" was the way you rebuilt boats;
rule of thumb used with our homes on sea.
Over-heard you tell so many "Who's the boss"-style jokes,
Sweetheart, as you made a queen of me.

Migrant Correspondence stayed with us on through the inland passage to Alaska.

Arriving there, we learned Alaska had its own home studies program and that we qualified. Once again we enrolled, but this time we had six students. We had a first grader!

They're the smartest kids in the world for six weeks, and every "matter-of-fact" is backed with, "Teacher said." Brady was that brain.

Brena, Bridget, Bart, Bunny and Brady,
Karate Class at Thomas Basin docks

Grandkids in Home School, San Jorge, Mexico, 2001

Home Studies/Rite or Rong

Alaska welcomed us that year, as summer dallied with the sun,
arriving at the Basin where the salmon season had begun.
We'd planned to stay just long enough to get acquainted with the town,
but harbor folks showed friendly air and welcomed us to stick around.
Construction work and crew aboard, would be some jobs for us to do.
First-rate correspondence studies would soon become our schooling, too.
Ten years spent in home-school cultures, scheduled round our family ties;
while teachers we'd grown fond of were replaced by ones in school disguise.
Old quote, "Don't fix something working,' drives agitators on until
a substitution has been found to wrong the right and cause ill-will.
This State's education system's remarkable controlled from home.
'Else we run the risk of raising bureaucrat-rats of our own!

There's one spot in the Northwest that's off the mainstream of Tongass Narrows in the "southeast" that wakes up our away-from-Alaska senses. Naha sits among the National Forest that seems to go on endlessly.

At its entrance are the private docks and very small native village of Loring. It is home to a once flourishing, but now old and abandoned cannery...history, just as the eye-catching house two friends, our juniors, enthusiastically built along its banks.

The STEAMER & our three other boats in tow, Tongass Narrows, Alaska

Naha can only be reached by boat or seaplane, but many of us felt it necessary to make the trip, often, some for summer camp; others for hiking; many for trout fishing in upper streams before netting their Sockeye at the Salt Chuck. But us...sheer pleasure!

Bart at Loring, Alaska

Naha/Northwest

A stone's throw out from Ketchikan lies Naha's inlaid map,
all nestled in a foggy bay just off the beaten path.
You step within her forests and are taken by surprise,
thick undergrowth that seems to cause a hush to make one wise.
The trees have fallen there and here. Their roots torn from the earth,
are spread with moss and vines and fern as carpet round their girth.
You're captured by an inner peace and, yet, uneasy feel.
To question all the beauty here makes some afraid and still.
Along the wooden man-made paths are berries in full-bloom.
Small wonder where the creatures are that come out to consume.
A salt-chuck keeps the bay from going up the creeks and streams
and separates the salty brine from water, fresh and clean.
The Sockeye take a part of both to head upstream to spawn
and leave behind their life at sea, as Northwest life goes on.

Tongass Narrows, Alaska

With our experiences on the "Hood" and then later turning our bow towards those colder Alaskan waters, plenty of ventures and lots of line-tugging had qualified and taught us the ropes of choice anchorages.

The boys on the
32′ "Cat" cruisin′
George Inlet, Alaska

Metla Katla, Alaska
Lars & B.B′s boat

Bucky and Rup,
fire arm drill,
Coon Cove, Alaska

On the Hook

O, what a splendid summer out from Ketchikan one year!
We stayed until the autumn winds blew Fall in, cold and clear.
We'd anchor in a shallow cove, or one declared the best;
where perhaps all the crabs were in, or one to show our guest.
It didn't cause that big a stir—discussions almost sin.
Depended on our appetite just where the hook dug in.
'Bout once a week we'd head for town to stock up on supplies,
to call the folks and check the mail, or buy some small surprise.
Just two of us would jump down in the skiff for one fast ride;
get errands done and catch them heading out the other side.
The kids all had their diving gear down to our three-year-old.
So, like a fish in water, they stayed wet without a cold.
Aquatic life had been an added bonus in our book,
but best times logged in mem'ry have been living on the hook.

At a very early age, Rett, our second son and third child had been labeled, "blood and gore" and, "an accident looking for a place to happen" by Rup's first cousin, Mackie. She'd spent not a few times lugging him up the hill to our house with blood oozing. A chair folded up on him while there, also, cutting his finger off at the tip. We rushed him into Vegas and the doctor sewed it back on. You might say that he cut his teeth on the mountain's side in Blue Diamond, Nevada.

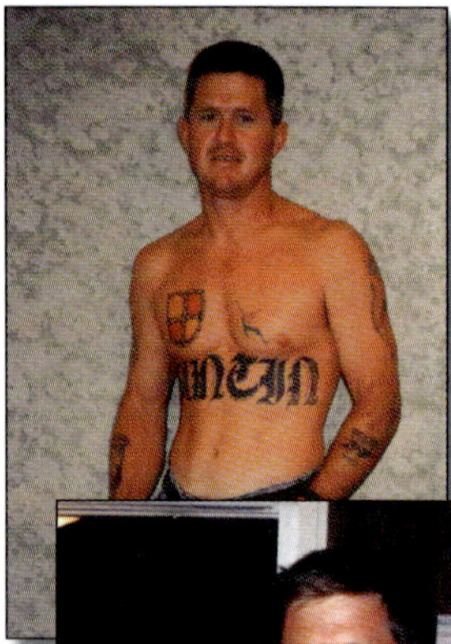

Years later in Bristol Bay, Alaska, on a gill-netter, he was in the engine room changing a belt. The captain carelessly turned on the engine and got that same finger. But this time his trip to the hospital was in a helicopter and this time he lost the finger. He joked with his dad later, "If you hadn't had that finger sewn back on, I wouldn't had to have that pain again."

Top: Rett

Middle:
Rett and his wife,
Cristina

Right:
Rett, Cristina and
children,
Pavy, Chapo and
Peggy

Rett/Steady

When he was a young kid he heard his dad say,
"That gang-plank, it leads to all parts, still, today."
Brought up on dad's heels, from a child, so he knew
that statement to some foe meant, "Who's stopping you?"
Respecting him greatly (no backup had he)
the attitude built in to man on the sea.
Plain lessons of learning were taught in those days:
to say what you mean and to mean what you say.
Since blessed with a nature of slight stubbornness,
this lad learned to use it to benefitness.
It's paid off on jobs that were tough tasks aboard
but when let go unchecked, nigh cut life's fine cord.
For like the wild Oak he's been raised hard, yet free.
Hard bent, yes, to do right but sometimes can't see.
Like any wild tree there's some pruning to get,
but after it smarts some, he's better for it.
So, duty-bound, son, hard as knots, built that way,
you'll come through life's storms cause you trust and obey.

Everyone kept growing and so did the need for more elbow room on a newly acquired, very ancient crabber.

In its heyday, this boat had been a top-of-the-line fishing vessel. But here we were, our third boat, though this time sizing it for fit.

Brent is the yard-arm monkey seen hanging from its mast, hammer in hand in the poem following. That hammer would one day be his trade mark.

Granny
STEAMER, Alaska

Time and Chance

Smack dab! in the dead of winter with Alaskans' windy storm,
he began to build a wheel-house with a stateroom for a dorm.
Soon the braver son was hanging, perched upon the highest point.
Down below, his brothers helped him nail the boards that form the joint.
Seems like "Pop" could ' used the weather of that gorgeous time in June.
But, somehow, it never happens—they keep working by the moon.
One 'wise-lad' found nerve to ask him, "How come projects never fail
bringing us ungodly-weather? Can't you plan 'round that detail?"
Dad said, "Time and chance I plan by." Lad was left without remark.
*"**Time** is wasting—let's get started. **Chance** we'll have it done by dark!"*
He has spent his life just teaching them the skills to build each need.
For he had them doing 'lay-out' by the time they learned to read.
Pushed them for an education, man's necessity in life,
but the type he chose for schooling was, far more, than read-n-rite.
There's no limit to their learned skills. Don't forget their sisters, too;
for they, too, worked on the engines, building boats and trikes, to boot.
So we never had great riches—taught them love and self-respect.
It's the gift, this side of Heaven, laced with wisdom that's the best.

Wished that Rup and I could always add "And they lived happily ever after." That comes when the family sticks to basic goals and remembers what is top priority. But only chaff to the wind if character isn't trimmed regularly and preparation for a tomorrow built-to daily.

The beginning years in San Jorge, Mexico. Tough times!

Hold or Fold

Mixed with cultured traits of his that
blended well with trends of hers
and then measured out eleven times in turn.
Salted with a life on sea and
spiced in home-taught sailor's lore
in our sea-quest, did each harbor what he'd learned?
Lessons taught to give and take designed around the school of knots
tied each sibling's friendship closer than the 'norm.'
As a two-fold cord will bond and pull
together when it's taut —
tight is how we seemed to weather every storm.
Now a wind of sorts is blowing cross
the oceans of each life,
as disturbance on the water starts to move;
while the warning summons each of you
to size-up family ties
and consider 'hold or fold' on basic views.
Brought up in a fashion "tough"
as work and play out-weighed the tears,
made the face of childhood often wear a smile.
Like a legacy unfolding —
heirlooms for a hundred years, customized,
you're just another Buntin child.

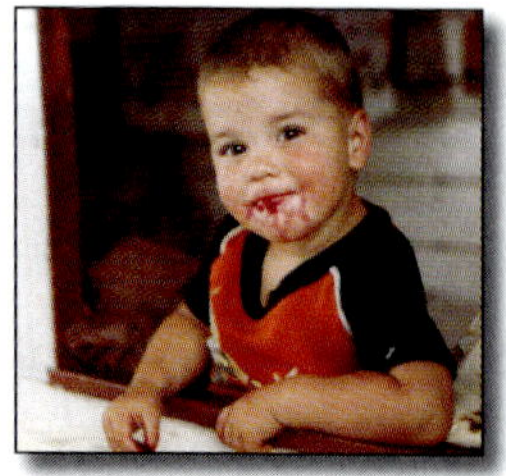

Brandy enjoys beets!

Brandy, our sixth son and second from youngest child has shared a kindred spirit with the salty sea since a bathtub experiment when an infant of two weeks old.

B.B., his sister and I were going to teach him to swim with this new babies-can-swim technique.

Brady, Brandy, Bucky, & Bo having a 'tote' on the back deck.

Everything was ready—except Mom! In I went! Now to slip slowly under with the baby. One look at that cute, tiny water-logged creature and out I came! Uh! Uh! No gracias!

Later he would pickup where I failed by extending his education along those lines with his certification and open water dive taking place in Prince William Sound, Alaska.

After dipping in the Northern Pacific, his instructor said he was now ready for any waters, anywhere.

Brandy has a second, or is it first, love for medicine, and has bought multiple books to benefit training in this relationship. We're the ones benefited, however, as he dives deeper into this art.

Brandy on Lookout

Brandy, Oleathia & Jenoá, today, Sea of Cortez, Mt. Point, Mexico

Brandy/Coon Cove

Custom dive suits, fins intact,
had been the family's treat.
The first chance out to some quiet cove
would make this gear complete.
We headed out—When weather broke
to find our favorite cove
and soon were ground-tied fast and snug
where we had always dove.
Our second youngest son was first
to break the surface waves
and didn't come on board that day
till all his siblings raved.
He'd never proved his wet gear in
the depths amidst the cold;
the unknown posed a challenge as he
went, this eight-year-old.
With pride we've each one made the choice
to live life on the deep,
but this son's choice goes deeper
for his heart dwells in the sea!

If we jump ship prematurely, the winds and the waves of life will take us away.

If we stay aboard faithfully, we'll arrive!

The Ship

The course already planned has plain and
simple rules for each.
This ship will not delay until its
destination's reached.
Was charted long before there was a
'you' to plot its run
and settled without help from 'me' to
reach the setting sun.
Disruptions aren't impossible, but
orders written, are.
Interference can't restrain the vessel
should some discord start.
The crew aboard will understand the
tight-ship's role at sea,
although the left, knows not the right hand,
still there's unity.
Command is clear, but one-on-one, yet
profits every mind.
Confirmation as a unit, oft
affirmed from time to time.
Discontention won't prevent or
mutiny the pre-planned trip,
nor harm the ones who've chosen 'stay on
board this HOME-BOUND SHIP!

Buck is our last child and seventh son. He never had a problem taking full advantage of being the youngest around his siblings.

Bucky, Ketchikan, Alaska

Although he's very quiet and terribly gentle, can hold his own in any crowd.

He latched onto a stray dog, lean and (mean?) looking for handouts years ago. Named him P.J. Before long the boy and his dog had the same personality.

Bucky, the teenager

P.J. and Bucky, Texas

Bucky/Gentle

Balanced on her knees he painted
pictures of some abstract scenes.
Maybe he would ask some questions,
"How come, Bun?" and, "Why?" of things.
Kindergarten and the First Grade
"she" took credit for his skill
with a special home-school honor
for the TOP KID. What a thrill!
After 'First,' the three girls took turns
with his schooling midst their own.
So he owes his love of reading
to his sisters' efforts shown.
If all kids had caused the problems
that this boy has caused for us,
there'd be minus teenage worries
for all parents, less the fuss.
Families tend to favor babies
even when they're six-foot tall.
In his case, he may not reach that,
but he's special to us all!

Let's have an affair — with Alaska, that is! Sea tramps could spend an eternity in its southeast region and never see it all.

From Skagway to the Dixon Entrance a pot of gold awaits each fisherman, logger, trapper, puddle-jumping pilot, people that live remotely recluse and cherish every waking moment, and then, **Sea Dogs....**

Stake a claim in this vast wilderness, but be prepared to deal with your greed. Mine, mine, mine!

And it is!

Tugboat anchored out in Metlakatla, Annette Island, Southeast Alaska

How we looked when we were traveling....1985

An Alaskan Affair

Summers in Alaska can be
awesome, less the rain;
welcomed though, brings forth our
breathless forests and terrain.
Inlets run away from straits and
form their own course, too.
Coves are weaned from them to make
a seaman's dream come true.
Fjords guarded by the cliffs,
majestic, sheer and tall.
Silence too protects and watches
near the moss grown wall.
Misty bays play quietly with
the beach if there's a calm,
hoping weary fishermen
will anchor till the dawn.
In this Southeast paradise,
that we can claim as home, we've
raised our kids to love this land
Alaska proudly owns!
A million years, they're not enough
to go where eagles dare.
The half cannot be told, for it's
a one-on-one affair!

Getting enough of shore duty has always let the highlight of boat life shine...untying the line!

Two of a Kind...

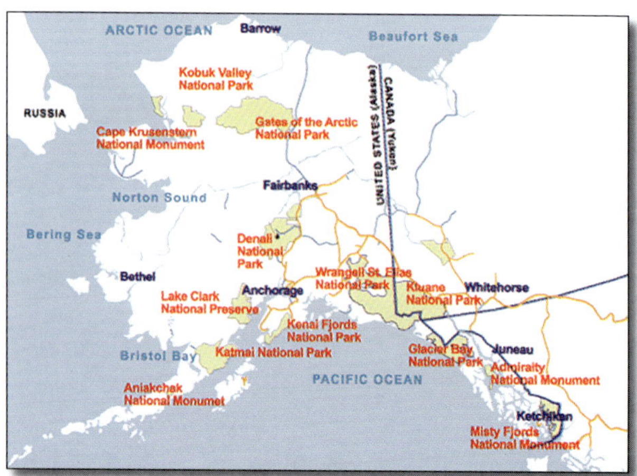

Two of a Kind

"Catch us if they can," our thoughts ran wild as we escaped,
leaving Ketchikan out past the levy's water break.
Too much city life is tough enough when there's a need,
not to mention shore line ties that grounded you and me.
So much undiscovered and new friendships that won't wait,
if perhaps we missed the boat, by chance had mustered late.
Still we're warned that rolling stones will not adhere to moss;
never felt a mossy back could ease our restless cause.
Two-of-a-kind, with prayers in sync, lines tied fast unrolled;
struggling free we've strayed some distance from the common fold.
Out here as the dolphins play their tag games with the bow,
and the pod of whales on farther blow at random now;
bits of sun and sand and sea brush cob webs to the wind;
salty air refreshing meanwhile two lives on the mend.

Sawdust swept up. Back deck scrubbed. Change in our pocket. This calm could only mean one thing... Rup has a plan! What makes it impossible to deal with is the encouragement he gets from the boys when they're not off somewhere salmon fishing.

The girls, too, with or without school assignments out of the way, coming to aid or humor him. What's the use? "If you can't lick them"...S'pose they have hovercraft information at the library?

Brandy, Brady and "Mom" at Thomas Basin, Alaska admiring their Hovercraft

Our newly built Hovercraft in Mexico, today... Southern style!

Hover Craft

We scanned the shelves for all-terrain, but source was sparse and skimp.
The lack of books and Lit on hand forced brochures to be sent.
So put together our best notes and improvised a draft,
then came up with a sweet design, a mocked-up hover craft.
Its large blades built astern were caged for safety, just in case.
Air from those lift fans, powered by Briggs, would fill the skirts to race.
With horse pow'r nearly twenty-four to give the launch a boost,
revved-up Zenoa was made the choice of engine brands he used.
Now launching day had finally come to give the tub a spin.
The pier held friends and kids, alike, to watch the test begin.
From where we stood, it seemed to dig below a wave and plow,
then jumped somehow propelled from sea and cleared that hole with pow'r.
Our friends all waved and cheered its feat, no longer just a raft,
but now instead a hover boat the triumph of this craft.
With transom dropped in tail-gate style, though that's another tale,
this boat could fly on board back deck; now, Hover Crafts, we hail!

STEAMER, Alaska

Skilled sailors and expert seamanship still become a drop in the bucket to the ocean throes. But for all this, mercy drops rule. When the weather broke for a moment between Southeast Alaska's notorious winter storms, we hurriedly hoisted anchor and made a mad dash into one of Ketchikan's marinas, Bar Harbor.

The fisherman watching from the cabin window of his Gillnetter was observing a family making "fast tracks" to dock, and that would, very soon, become a close friend and participant of the fishing fleet on his dock.

Lending a helpful hand he was quite amused with the likes of this captain and crew; and the number of "hands" that kept showing up on deck. This salmon fisherman introduced himself to this water logged crew as, B.J.

Inside the STEAMER

Chain of Command

From out of nowhere they appeared with mooring lines in hand.
The boys were drenched but still alert to hear their dad's command.
Up in the wheel house you could see his stern face calculate,
though wind and wave and sea gone mad, to dock or yet to wait.
Down through a porthole one could glimpse their mother rushing 'round,
securing food upon the stove while sitting baby down.
One girl was in there doing her share of keeping him below,
while on the stern, two others stood prepared with lines to throw.
At last the signal pierced the night to, "Nab it at first try!"
He felt there'd be no second chance, to miss would be to die!
For eighteen years they've lived aboard and each time in a Blow,
the thought that's shared by all of them, "Is this our time to go?"
While current and swells fight for control, the tide against them turns,
but trust in dad and faith in God, the courage within them burns!
Soon, boats secured and safely tied. Each person whispers, "Thanks!"
With years they've learned, although they're skilled,
He holds the highest rank.

Swinging from the anchor in a special cove would make a temporary home during the summer months in Alaska. Every now and then we'd catch a little tale about a strange wind that could come straight down a mountain-side and sit on you. That seemed weird! Because we thought mountains were for protection, a place to tuck behind and hide from the wind. Coon Cove was the safe spot we'd chosen for this trip. We were greenhorns! We sure aren't now. Doubt if that particular Wind ever was!

Coon Cove, Alaska — Tied to a log boom

Williwaw

Perhaps you've felt tornadoes
and have read about cyclones,
but we can tell you of a wind
that isn't that well known.
One night we all were fast asleep
while anchored in a cove;
as we had spent a hard day
catching food for which we dove.
Some cukes, and crab and bottom fish,
a gourmet sea delight.
Yes, just another day of liv-
ing close to nature right.
We don't know where it came from
as it caught us unprepared.
But in the darkness of that night
we felt so strangely scared.
This force unseen but oh so real
hard-pressed our boat from top.
With power to push it to the depths,
we felt it'd never stop.
Quick as we tried to find our wit
and gain the upper hand,
this power-lust force was holding us
to port by its command.
As quickly as it came, it went!
And we were left in awe!
Each staggered forth to give salute
to our first WILLIWAW!

After a few years in Alaska, the boys and their dad sent for an ultralite kit.

I was too busy. Had kids to raise. School to teach, meals cooking, so somehow they got past me and my opinion on this one. Little did I know that I would soon be up to my elbows in glue and gunk!

Footnote: Have you ironed a wingtip, lately?

B-Ten Ultra Lite on floats

B-Ten Ultra Lite

Fifteen foot of back deck space with room to walk between
became the shop for two fine Wings of fabricated skein.
Thirty-two would be their length, in feet, together spanned,
but who'd have known the major task when we had sent for plans?
Purchase of a kit in hopes assembling, quick, seemed wise,
unprepared for what "kit" meant revealed our big surprise!
Packaged tough and sure in case the shipping got too hard,
unveiled boards direct from Mills we'd sooner bought from Yards.
Improvising, seemed to rule with each print from the kit.
Building Baby Grands would take us less time, we'd admit.
Long before this ultra lite was floating in the bay,
Rup had engineered each part, a B-Ten built his way.
Now we're gun-shy when it comes to building from a kit.
All we'd wanted was a chance to ***fly****, not* ***invent,*** *it!*

Sure things can come back and bite. Be careful when you bet on them; as Lars discovered in a card trick Rup played on him once. Rup laid several rows of cards out. He had Lars pick one without showing him. On purpose, Rup dealt past the one he knew Lars had picked. Then Rup said, "O.K., your card will be the next card I turn over." With that said, Lars exclaimed, "That's a sure thing!" Then Rup reached back up the row and flipped Lars' card over. Total surprise!

To make the following story shorter, do you think a girl would propose to a guy if she didn't already know the answer?

Once Upon a Time

Once upon a time a guy and gal fell both in love.

A story to be told had just begun.

"Be fruitful, multiply," would bring them blessings from above,

eleven children, seven of them sons.

Their daughters each were marked with beauty, salted with delight,

just like a sailor's ship, she makes him glad.

Given four, they'd been rewarded with these lovely sights,

and apples of the eye for any dad.

The yarn about these two would not influence but just a few,

unless the easy chair become a bore;

for never can one feel or touch the edge the way they do,

until he gives up clinging to the shore.

This family, reared-to-ramble, has exceeded boundary's line;

tradition screaming loudest to retreat.

Not to worry, for still they toil while trying to keep time

to the ocean's sentimental beat.

Friends on boats exchanged their notes in San Francisco Bay

while talking, walking, working with each tide.

But fishing northern waters on up Alaska way

caught hold like gold rush fever's lucky strike.

The folklore doesn't end, they smell each rose that's handed them.

An odyssey that providence still leads.

They'll happ'ly live adventure as each fairy tale begins,

for once upon a time a gal proposed; the guy agreed!

Anyone that has met Rup doesn't need me to mention that he nearly always has some sort of goings-on, going on. His timing to build this first of two trikes is not traditional! It doesn't seem to phase any member of this darn family. Can't we be just a teensy-bit civilized?

Rup and Carrol's trikes
Tongass Narrows, Ketchikan, Alaska

Traditional Wedding?

Weddings always make us cry. Just why, I don't know why.
Could be b'cause we gain instead of shrink in family size.
Was in the eve of one of ours, a Bug would take new life,
the back deck spread with tools and grease would soon produce a "Trike."
We launched it on the dock and found it tested true and sound,
so, grabbed our youngest son of ten and then were Texas-bound.
Looking in the rearview as we cleared the off-ramp way,
Alaska's link to us was just its Ferry in the bay.
We headed cross the country with a million miles to go
and felt the freedom of the road that bikers only know.
His yellow Trike and mine of, blue, were sure to cause a scene,
but more a treat to passerbys, the boy in back they seen.
Would be a task to choose which State that out-shone all the rest,
for each and everyone had parts that were the very best.
Ask us why we crossed each State by Trikes to see the sights?
Maybe for the same cause Trikes are built on wedding nights.

On a good ship, there is
no human as grateful
as the one rescued.

Red Snapper — Brent and Lars fishing in Hood Canal
out of Hadlock, Washington

Salted Breed

Heave to thar young mateys and gather 'round me.

Come hearken to what I've to say.

There's many a sailor who's lost out at sea.

By jove! Trained you are for this day.

They can't see the light house, they've drifted too far.

Poor souls never learned how to swim.

With sea legs, you're gifted by compass and star;

step lively, now use 'em for them.

Their cry comes in earshot. The deep calls them home.

Heave ho, lads, take heed as you go.

You bloody well know, that your lives aren't your own.

You am what you am! Make it show!

When ship wreck has forced fear and anguish of soul,

all hope's torn completely away.

Be brave hale and hearty, their lives you might hold.

Aye, fellows be wise to obey.

A land lubber's fate left to chums on the shore,

nay, salt ne'r has mixed in their veins.

Hang tight to your mooring, naught with them you'll score.

You're made of the breed you sustain.

I have a complaint! First off, I'm aware that there must be **sacrifices** made to live aboard and that the alternative has a way of helping you make up your mind—lighten the burden, or sink!

Now I, the expert, know space is **sacred.** There are some **gifts** that can't be put on the **altar** when it comes to this load-lightening.

My only complaint: How come all Rup's contraptions remain a part of family **doctrine,** but mine are tossed **overboard?**

Gyro

Gyrocopter...and my missing bowl

Well, Bowl Me Over!

Mind slips me now of all the junk we've stowed down through the years.
At least it was to me, but held in high esteem by seers.
I've had to eat my humble pie quite often in this clan.
Time never gets too far ahead before a new craft's planned.
Was long ago, down near Mt. Hood, Rup had a pin machined
and kept it 'round for oh! so long. Now, what had Einstein schemed?
Large blades were scraped and cleaned with wheels once used to roll a cart,
and sheets of tin from who knows where, few clues to this upstart.
But when I missed my galley bowl…the set was stainless steel,
aha! I knew some cards were played and mine, a dirty deal!
His oath to soon replace the set, to which I only laughed,
is still on hold! That bowl's the nose cone on his rotor craft!

I'll admit I'm Irish. Have overcome blackcats and walking under ladder superstitions. Please allow me to play around with the prophetical course Rup's grandfather must have surely foreseen when living in the middle of Texas he nicknamed his grandson STEAMBOAT. The ocean was just a Big Pond somewhere out West past the Rockies, that neither had seen!

Rupert Sr., Mom, and Rup
San Diego, California

Many years later on a train bound for San Diego and Boot Camp, that "Pond" came in view. Rup exclaimed, "What's that?" His buddy drawled, "The Mississippi River, dumb ass!"

Rup and Pa on the farm in Texas

Pa, Papa and Dad

The Buntins' B-half-circle crest
claimed as the family's brand,
past down from Pa, our great grandad,
a Texas cattleman.
His oldest son, our Papa now,
broke horses, then, for pay.
Fact, Granny's wedding ring was bought
from bucks earned in that way.
Pa's grandson, dad, was his side-kick,
dubbed STEAMBOAT, pep and steam.
With calf rope lost on Pa's scared calf,
child's guilt hoped he'd not seen.
Alas, the ocean chanted tales.
Its music stirred his mind;
donned bottoms, bell, in trousers; blue,
left Texas far behind.
Years later in ole STEAMER'S hull,
dad built a stove and hearth
with B-half-circle branded in
the hearthstone fire wall guard.
Might take a lad from Texas, now.
Dad's happy on the sea.
But never take the Texas from
his branded family tree!

Aunt Callie had lived out West a long, long time. We had come to live with her when I was six and had stayed around her and Uncle Red "pretty close" for the rest of my adolescent years. She was always more of a Grandmother figure to us than an aunt and pillaging her "cookie jar" is one of my favorite memories.

The highlight of our visit with Aunt Callie was her excitement when she realized Rup was there when he leaned over to kiss her.

We're not complete without some of the old paths to follow.

Aunt Callie

Dear Lady

She sits, dear little lady, over
near the window there,
all wrapped up in her thoughts while
nestled in an easy chair.
Seems curtains of the past unroll
as scenes come to her mind,
and she attempts to sort them out
while occupying time.
Soft, tiny hands unfold as kindred
voices reach her ears;
life's hastened loss of hearing
hasn't hindered family cheer.
Though twilight years have come to stay
and shades her sight from glare,
those Irish eyes still twinkle through
the glasses that she wears.
With love that never needed questioned
and a smile, sincere,
her pantry door remained unlocked,
for us, throughout the years.
Our visit with Aunt Callie
makes us treasure by gone days.
Now for us, two, life's richer,
honey, in old-fashioned ways.

More time on hand to ponder personal thoughts about what's coming in through the city's gate.

Grand-daughter, Lillian Maria, all dressed up!

Unattained Age

And as she stepped in sis's shoes, the heels she'd one day fill,
and folded twice the skirt to fit her length in grown-up frills;
with make-up splattered cross her face, her mirror looked back amazed
reflecting acts of childhood that another child has played.
Youth has a threshold to be crossed with age respecting none;
though nature seems to favor young, still different for each one.
There seems to be no problem with the natural flow of life
but taking on responsive acts, this action many fight.
So, parents foot the bill to teach and train their own child well,
in hopes he'll 'stand on his' one day, accountable to self.
But take account of actions shown and size up all this mess;
some so-to-speak, old teens have turned their backs on grown up dress.
I question just how many back step when they've reached full term
and never do they quite attain to hold adulthood, firm.
Still, making that decision is one's choice, we all know well.
Sure glad I'm not the BIG JUDGE, I'd send half these kids to…jail!

My father brought us out west from Georgia, after first grade, to Hunt, Idaho. This had been a internment camp for American citizens a few years prior to our arrival. I will mention, once more, proudly that the best friend that Rup and I ever had was of Japanese origin.

Rup's Honda V-65 Magna with side car

Graduation from Twin Falls High and moving on after marriage, would see my hometown transformed by the expansion boom while destroying many childhood memories.

Bikin' Cross Time

I lived here once, was long ago,

or was that someone else?

Two different lives, two different roads,

my heart within me melts.

We drive down streets, now strangers claim,

down lanes while memory clears.

Nostalgia plays its ghost-like games.

Reality fights tears.

It hurts to come back to the start,

'cause home's not here today.

You took my hand; I won your heart;

life's trail led us away.

Rev up your bike, kick up the stand,

the past must keep its own.

In silence, let me grieve this land,

the place I once called home.

The wind, our friend, feels free as we

make tracks across past times.

I'll not look back; ahead's the sea.

Thanks, hon, you made it mine!

At the end of the salmon season in Ketchikan, Rett, Brent and Brady, Cristina and Bunny headed out to Baja to visit Cristina's family. Murphy's Law stopped them in Everett, WA., for a major overhaul on one of the two pickups, Chevy and Ford. After finding a friend's vacant shop they began to operate.

Cabo San Lucas at Sleepy's house: Juan, Bucky (fresh out of Alaska), Bunny Bee, Brady, Rup and Ruppy with Sue inside

They took the body off the Ford's firewall forward; same to the Chevy. Cut the frame behind the two transmissions, removing both, still mounted to the front frame. Then slid smaller Chevy frame inside Ford frame and welded them up. It still had the transmission, engine, radiator, front suspension and steering wheel. They put the Ford fenders, hood and grill back on Chevy frame, now a part of the Ford. They cut the drive-lines in two, welding the Chevy's front to the Ford's back.

Overhaul completed, new owners of one "CheFord."

All of this happened before reaching the beautiful white beaches near Cabo San Lucas and a Gringo called "Sleepy."

Sleepy

We met a man from Californ'
an heir of Alabam',
and he a thousand miles from
home on Lower Baja sand.
Acquaintance came about when southland
surfaced just enough
to let his Dixie traits conceal
his California stuff.
A bachelor in his younger years
that gals could not resist;
while debonair, an easy-catch
when he met up with Chris.
Their welcome mat intended for
more than one's dirty feet,
this couple's hands' extended
hospitality indeed!
Devices he invented helps
their son fulfill his call;
perhaps with greater pride than
need had not been there at all.
Performance of his "Sam McGee"
takes back-row seat to none
but best of Sleepy's peevish quips:
"Youth's wasted on the young!"

The rainfall in Ketchikan is from 160″ to 200,″ yearly. Learning to dodge the raindrops and the blahs is a community success, cause everywhere there's pleased Alaskans as everywhere there's scurrying.

But when the wind blows gale force, the rain continues for three weeks without a sign of let-up; four leaks untraceable in the galley, we've got cabin fever!

Sue and Ruppy in San Carlos, Mexico, relieving that "itch" by purchasing our first huge Dive Compressor from Club-Med

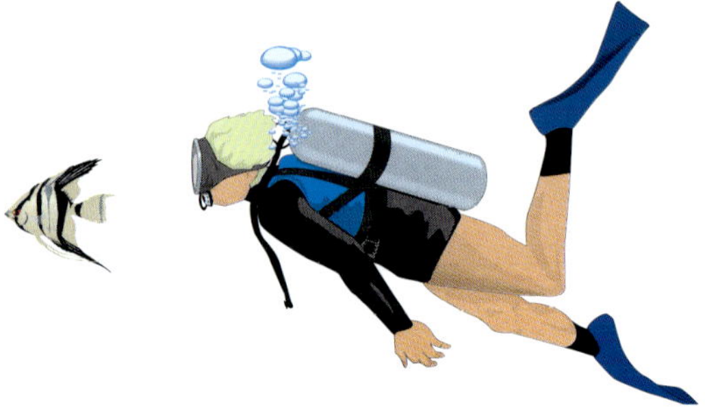

Southern Itch

Warned you not to hug the Border;
not to get too close;
not to hum "South of the Border"
tune enticed us both.
Cabin fever in Alaska
got us on the run.
What relief, this side of Shasta,
when we felt the sun.
Broken down in Arizona
headed for the farm;
desert air made five day shut down,
tempt with Spanish charm.
How we ever made El Paso,
sick from blues inside!
Had to vow we'd someday, both go
cross the border, side.
Mexicano flair of music,
down-home style of life,
just a start of relived childhood
that you thought I'd like.
Itch to go kept taunting big-time.
State side's cure too slow.
Packed belongings, boats, the meantime.
Hola, Mexico!

On one of our, almost monthly, trips from Old Mexico to Texas we had gotten through Van Horn without mishap. If there were to be trouble or break-downs, it happened in that town.

By the time we reached Pecos, one of those renown West Texas sand storms was kicking up its heels.

During the blindness, I remembered our never-pain-free friend's solution to typical situations. Jann's remedy: If life gives you lemons, make lemonade.

My cue to write a few worthy words about the "Great State of Texas".... Ahem!...

Pardners

Bluebonnets are sonnets arranged by the Pro.
Although, we can pick them, we can't make them grow.
A classic creation in wind blown attire,
all dressed up in flocks for the Mockingbird's choir.
These masters of mimic make mockery of all,
by counterfeit bragging to show off their drawl!
Spring's early bird songsters smirk night and day chimes
to usher in Scissor tails, one of a kind.
Officials, assuring that Spring's really sprung,
perhaps, by their forked tail or someone's forked tongue.
What matters, they keep Flies off Texas' Long Horn,
no equal's been found since the day he was born!
The tougher they are, makes the rougher they fall.
Oh, mercy me! Who'd dare push him at all?
Endurance was taught him by West Texas Storms,
the Dust Bowl for sand thrown when weather gets warm.
If Pecos remains when Dust Devils spin through,
its dirt will return by the Panhandle's Crew.
Can't tell if they're Fables, or Fibs, or if Truths,
just "Don't Mess With Texas," they're all in cahoots!

Continuing our trip as the dust settled and leaving Texas still on the map, we knew from the oil rig count, pump-jack watch and that, uh, smell that we were passing through the Permian Basin.

Soon, though, Mesquite thickets were replaced by Live Oak, as wild Bluebonnets began multiplying along the freeway's median. We knew we were nearing the peanut country and the farm.

State of Mind

The "Yellow Rose's" not all that grows, and grows from Texan notes.

The roster's spilt the beans of many names.

And should some spark one's interest in their treasured, Alamo,

his bended ear could never be the same.

The banners States saluted when each one by one took stands,

with standards they would set at frontier's door;

would wave in many colors in this Southern Tex/Mex land,

as Six-Flags flew the different shades it wore.

The Lone Star man I married cut his teeth on Jack knife rigs,

was long before I knew the price of oil.

Fascinated me how children grew up Texas, big.

My guess, their place in history and its soil.

Admiring upright values lived by some the way they see

would move us to impart choice views to ours.

So didn't feel it strange to add a pinch of Texas T,

that mix of rebel pride inspired with power.

Out on the sea we've brushed and touched with men of many views

and feel out there Beyond the Sea, that's next,

at Round-Up time there'll surely be an answer from a few

when Roll is taken and He calls out, "Tex!"

Hiding from the hot breath of the Cortez Sea, Brena and her dad enjoyed reminiscing about the fishing harbors of Alaska and almost catching a whiff of the nets strung along the docks there. We laughed about the times the girls and I had caught our shoe heels in the them as we jumped from one fisherman's net to the next. We tried to avoid the entanglement but our boat was docked at the end of this lead.

Bar Harbor, Alaska, STEAMER

The Fishermen were good natured and they would tease about us being "keepers," or swear that they always keep what they catch. It was always fun greeting the returning fleet after a prosperous trip. Furthermore, we had investments in it! Rett also had a gill netter.

Brena & Davey

Brena, "Little Sister" in the following poem has two children today: Sam and Davey.

Davey & Sam

Davey, Brena's son

Sam, Brena's girl

Tide Change

Little sister, do you miss the many sounds in harbors, past?
And your brothers, do they crave to hear the gulls;
hear the clanging of the halyard lines against the neighbor's mast,
as the changing tide slaps lightly on the hulls?
Can you almost smell the fishing boats that tied up down the dock,
and remember how they sidled-up like rafts;
when, "Hey, let 'er blow!" was echoed through the fleet as one man mocked;
how his unconcern made skippers later laugh?
Older sisters, do you think they miss their bunks on board back then,
rocking gently as our boat gave into swells;
with imaginations drifting, sounds of creaking planks from wind,
as it whistled, gusting through the sheets and sails?
Since we've left the northern ports along Pacific's inland pass,
lonesome whispers stir our memories, now and then.
Harbor hopping's got a magic geared to sailors, but alas!
ventures, sis, must bid "adieu" as those times end.

Since the day Rup and I drug Mom and Dad to the chapel she's made me part of the family. Having just the one son and him pushing-thirty made it look hopeless for her as far as grandchildren went. More than a handful would one day be hers.

Birthday! Carrol, Dad and Mom Buntin
Gorman, Texas, 1960

Mom

There's a place beside the two of us and it belongs to you.
From the start it was prepared you occupy, though God just knew.
Britches mended by you from his scrapes and falls when just a youth.
Switches used, instilled instructions. Once you 'wrestled' for his tooth!
Can I really, ever, thank you for the way you raised your son?
Maybe not, but I'll keep using those fine tactics with our own.
Someday, if our girls are lucky, and our boys stay well aware,
they'll be welcomed in some family or take someone in as theirs.
Through the years you've stayed a "lady" while you refined motherhood,
and your grand-kids are a witness that you're Grand at being good.
But for me to share your birthdate always tickled us so much
and I'd like to think that was the way He gave his final touch.

Ruts are paths that are easily slipped into and often hard to be freed from.

Rup, today, on our boat, "Ol' Reb" the "CAT" outside La Pinta, Mexico

Spartan Souls

The little thoughts I've conjured up before we cross the Pond;
so proud his visionary schemes have pushed this family on.
Quite often people come to mind who'd benefit like us,
but more than often there's a reason that they won't discuss.
Seems tunnel vision, narrowly kept, inhibits many eyes,
and prison binds the Spartan soul from ventures once deemed wise.
If bondage is the trendy dress for those who've courage, sold,
no matter, one can change attire when he turns from its hold.
Old standards, proud saluted have been lowered so for mobs.
Price purple hearts and medals now. Did heroes die for naught?
Make freedom ring and turn about; why box up your extremes?
Bring someday near within arms reach and live those out-there dreams.
And why bow down to "wood and stone" to search utopia's glee?
For there's a million lands to roam with space spun endlessly.
To live without a vision wouldn't feel like life was whole.
We're looking for our voyage, soon, out past that yonder shoal.

After Dad was gone a year the family gathered at his Texas farm and began construction of boats. It was a carpenter's field day, with the crew size numbering twenty counting Granny. There would soon be eight boat hulls scattered around this port-less farm.

Bart later put music to this poem. We miss Dad!

The Catamaran Farm, Gorman, Texas

Dad's Farm Port

Of course it raised the neighbors' brows and tongues sure wagged in town,
as back out on his farm news of our project got around.
Within a space of time that some would swears a Texas yarn,
we'd built four boats with double hulls and misfit Papa's farm.
We'd long ago exhausted shocking him in any way,
for in his later years he'd only shrug and often say,
"I see it working for you, son. Be last to flat deny.
But I just can't retrain myself; it scares me…ain't no lie."
He'd watched us raise his grandkids on a boat with great delight,
and always marveled how protection came in strange disguise.
We've hauled each boat now, one by one, to sea for testing skills;
observed as each outdone our hopes, plus whet our mounting thrills!
But every now and then we glimpse a thought that makes us glad
and feel that somewhere out there waits a shrug from dear ole dad.

Photos are expensive but
mind's photography is priceless.

Sunset over the Sea of Cortez, Mexico

Are You Listening?

Winds across the sea
enhanced with sunlight's savory gleams
rush shimmering beads of
sparkles that dance cross the ocean streams.
Photos fail to capture
all the magic of these kinds;
keepsakes treasured,
and won't fade in closets of our minds.
Living on the edge
will let events in nature's scenes
focus one on simple arts
that some folks miss, it seems.
Take away the challenge
of each open door in life,
we'd miss an opportune
time for peace from stress and strife.
Caught up in life's cares
makes nature hard to understand.
Putting life on hold,
alas, the curse of mortal man.
Daydreams come to life
when we put feet to dreams we've stalled.
Have a purpose lest
you faint and answer wakeup's call.

Old Mexico at last! To have found an ideal spot to launch our boats was almost too good to be true. Seven miles out of Puerto Penasco (Rocky Point) at an oyster farm, we had met a middle aged Mexican couple who gave us permission to set up a makeshift camp behind their cottage. We could finally put those three boats to the test. Would they float? We'd soon see.

The "Cats" we built and hauled from Texas

Heading out to the sea at La Pinta, 20 miles from Rocky Point, MX. Our "Cat" was remodeled for a friend, and along for the trip was our boys' old dive boat.

Getting ready for a Sunset Cruise coming out of the Harbor at Rocky Point on the "Morris", today

The Sea At Rocky Point

Ostionés on the beach.
Waves roll softly in.
Gentés working all day long;
sometimes without end.
A way of life, to work, to play
with little else to do.
But life goes on and on ý on,
and they're quite happy too.
When I complain because of heat,
or gripe for lack of funds,
can't help but shame myself a bit.
What choice have they to run?
Ah Mexico, with barren lands and
deserts near the sea.
Oh how I love you, my kind friend,
sweet peace and tranquil'ty.
Don't let me rob the ones who've braved
the hard times in this place;
nor hide my eyes from that dear man
who gathers cans for pay.
My heart will always leap within
each time I hear songs sung
by Mariachis in the square
exciting everyone.
Listen carefully to the folk,
not knowing what they say.
Who cares? It's pretty just the same.
I'll learn it too one day.

In Ketchikan, during a routine checkup at the dentist office information was exchanged with the doctor and I about good fishing spots and places to cruise. He mentioned a little fishing village below the Arizona Line on the Sea of Cortez. I hadn't the foggiest idea how soon this conversation would influence my family's life!

Sea of Cortez

On the south side of the border
near the north end of the Sea,
Cortez whispers to my spirit,
"Here's where rebels ought to be!"
It's this wandering spirit that's caused
a lot of turmoil in our life.
As they've tried to make us settle,
we've kept running from the strife.
Oh, I'm sure there'll always be some
as we go from place to place;
but nothing like we leave behind us
and to turn back's our disgrace.
There's a wild and haunting craze
that comes from listening to the Sea
and while watching as each wave that
breaks and somehow beckons me.
It's a beauty once you've seen it,
doesn't leave you ne'r the same;
and you know that others heed it,
for they too are called by name.
"Is the Sea a rebel," you ask,
"with a spirit we can't tame?"
But of course! It's quite tempestuous!
Yet we love it just the same.

Construction of boat hulls while keeping watch on the two already afloat, had half-hitched us to land and sea. Sand in the bed at night with very few places to hide from the sun during the day did try the nerves of a twenty year old, occasionally. Brady is our fifth son and ninth in the lineup and had been trying out flamenco style

music for nigh two years. Doing excellent, from his folks' point of view. So why the slumped shoulders?

Brady and Brenda

Brenda and Brady, Jr.

Brady

Don't hang your harp up, son, not now. Some man may have a need.
You've had some lows before in life. The goal's the same…proceed.
Don't hang your harp up. It's your song. Without it you would die.
You owe that gift of melody to others such as 'I'.
For feeble hands hung down, your blessed with gifted hands to play;
also, for hearts that need a change…don't put your harp away!
The willow has no need of it. But far too many do.
So take heart, son, lift up yourself and we'll be picked up too.
You're taught to be somewhat put out. Their comforts come first too.
Your gift to them, be as it should, a burden first to you.
Some things you take by faith that's blind when forced to carry on.
Remember that it's hard to see well just before the dawn.
Don't hang that harp up anymore. Your song of life still brings
a joy to us with your guitar on classic lively strings.

One day Rup and I were having coffee while watching Bunny serve refills to two of her regulars at the GALLEY in Ketchikan. These brothers, senior citizens, were complimenting her, “This coffee’s the best we’ve had all day.” Bunny replied,

“It should be, I strained it through my socks.”

Babette Billie “B.B.”,
Bunny Bee,
Bridget Bobbie,
and Brena Belle,
Carson, Washington
1975

Pleasant Harbor,
Washington
1978

Brena, Bridget, B.B.,
and Bunny,
Ketchikan, Alaska
1981

Brena, Bridget,
B.B. and Bunny,
Kona, Hawaii
1998

Cuatrós Hermanás

Portraits found in family albums frame a prim and proper pose.
Sisters to the core, these four, quite often shared their dreams and clothes.
Growing up at home they learned to go that extra mile or few;
pouring up another refill for some guest they catered to.
Turning cheek in situations was a part of family tact;
though at times was used to take aim with the eye that wasn't black.
Waiting tables down in Texas while sweet back home memories drift;
serving coffee hot, rejoicing, that their swing's not graveyard shift.
This vocation touches home base for they've watched old ethics stick.
Thankful dad applied some ground rules, as they count each coffee tip.
Waters of the Blue Pacific led astray their folks to roam,
so they lived Alaska's good life on the boat dad built as home.
Naturally the trays get heavy serving orders with hors d'oeuvres;
filling cups, they almost hear mom, "To be queen, first learn to serve."
Waiting tables down in Texas, holding tight to prayers within
and the Stranger's one day promise…He'll wait tables spread for them.

Campfires are essential to these aquatic gypsies. Before she was six weeks, Rup and I were dipping our first child, B.B., in the cold clear stream along the Big Wood's banks of Idaho. As the soot thickened on the coffee pot, Rup dreamed about that big trout soaking for tomorrow's catch.

Tide flats,
San Jorge, Mexico

Rupert, Sr.
Thomas Basin, Alaska
True cod, rare!

Gone Fishing

We fished the winding River of the
Snake, in Idaho…
a plate of Rainbow Trout was well rewarding,
and camped at Big Wood River with its
streams like polished gold,
the favored campsite gone from last reporting.
We left this Magic Valley for Pacific's
indigo,
with reels of happy times tucked safe inside us;
and found the ocean brimming full of
recipes to know
and grills of sea caught meals in many sizes.
Our men would work from sun to sun
but 'round the clock to fish.
At times that was the family's sole supporting.
We'd watch as tourists baited hooks
to bag their trophy wish
but never comprehended fish for sporting.
Have wound up wadding shorelines in the
Sea of Mexico,
as all the mud flat sea life spout with squishin'.
We're glad that anglers fever hung
around since Idaho…
for just when life's unruly we go fishin'.

Rup, Mom, Little Mom, B.B. & Rachael
Five Generations

As we travel the freeways and back roads of Arizona today, 'snowbirds' roam in every style R.V. imaginable. Bumper stickers displayed most frequently are: We're Spending Our Children's Inheritance. This prompted me to reevaluate our own children's future wealth and inheritance.

Brent already making use of his inheritance:
Overlooking Lake Tahoe, Nevada, from Incline Village area

Our Children's Inheritance

Absent without leave from sea
much longer than we'd planned
but re-discovered why the tide returns.
Even when we've had our fill
of fun while on the lam,
the shore holds back that life of freedom learned.
Tattooed in our minds with marks
unfaded, no remorse,
though scars nigh washed away to Davy Jones;
baptized in the fire of trials
on ocean's altered course,
we've wielded life like knives cut to the bone.
Quenching thirst and soothing souls
of children born to us,
by letting each partake of wealth we've seized;
pirate-like, with treasure found
we share with them this trust:
Four winds, inherit, and the Seven Seas.

While the outward properties of a tumbleweed are hard to be respected, I wonder if the man who wrote the country song, "Tumbling, Tumbleweed," was a mite envious of its disregard for the tied-down lifestyles?

Speaking of country music, Rup met Hank Williams when he passed through Rup's hometown of Gorman, Texas in the Forty's. Mr. Williams called him over and asked, "Hey, sonny, do you know why a rabbit's nose isn't shiny? Cause it has a powder puff on the other end."

Boat-building
Brena and Davey,
San Jorge, Mexico

Restless Rogues

Tumbleweeds detached, unwanted,
dried up from the heat and sand,
claim the wind as bosom buddies
as they take off cross the land.
Cacti reaching out like brothers;
sand dunes hasten their escape,
running free on desert dry plains…
not a chance they'll soon abate.
Parched and dusty without water
since they left their steadfast home,
but the urge to keep on rolling
makes these wanderers forced to roam.
Harmless yet with so much freedom…
takes so little from the earth,
sometimes envy twangs the heart strings
of poor souls tied fast to turf.
Motionless now wind's departed
leaving tumbleweeds ashore.
Unattached though still not hopeless…
time has always one more door.
Like these rogues, we've ceased from running
as the wind's gone from our sails.
In our wayward ways we'll stay low
till the wind picks up our trail.

When we got the green light from the border patrol we knew we were home free. Time flies when you're having fun, so it was and we were.

Our move out further to San Jorge would see lots of good times mixed with lots of hard work the following year.

Out in that desert we had a defiant one hid in its sand. He had the advantage and he had diner√≥. This little man was a giant. He was the type of friend we dare not turn our back on. This friend was a foe.

San Jorge, Mexico

Captain of the Host

Ask that man who stands with sword drawn near the outpost of our camp
if he's there for us avenging, or the adversary's Champ.
"Pase," from the border guard had led us home to this new land
but reproach and uninvited snares entrap our desert sand.
Why should we lay down our weapons, turning-tail for fear of giants?
True, though inside doubters threaten, bold delight outside's d'fiant.
Heard if one could whip a thousand, given two…ten-thousand run.
Strength in number, family's trump card, undivided…battle's won.
See the door? It's kept from closing. Shouldn't that nudge waning zeal,
over throwing mind's own logic, using faith instead of feel?
"Sir, make known ' us your position. Should we now defend our Post?"
"Loose thy shoe," He speaks. I tremble! For us…Captain of the host!

We should have taken a miner's view of the desert's floor that reaches 200 degrees in the Sonoran Desert. The entire family was anxiously awaiting the warm sands to soothe the dry rot and mildew that the Rain Forest of Alaska had inflicted. So a breeze from the sky-blue ocean would be a balm on the hottest of days…wrong!

Pouring cement in Hot, Hot sun, with "fake" conference taking place

Sue, Davey, Sam, Chapo and Pavy... Just poured the Pela on a hot day!

Down…Mexico Way

Another day in paradise.
I think we're gonna die!
The wind has ceased, the breeze is gone
and it's a record high.
Perhaps we missed the boat this time.
The compass needle lied.
Humidity is climbing fast.
The clouds left with the tide.
We've made some moves to last frontiers;
some towns were heaven sent.
When we came down here to this place,
guess… down… we really meant.
The ruff and tuff all get by here.
I'm not sure where we stand.
Quite sure our skin is ruff enough
with tuff hide gettin' tanned.
But one sweet night the cool wind blew.
The breeze felt oh so soft!
We fell back on our beds to dream.
Mosquitoes took us off!
So when you're bored and life gets dull,
you need to move around.
Just hop the next boat headed South,
and, SUCKER, come on down!

Exchanging one sea for another, plus another world too, was understated bliss.

The adoption of Mexico, or versa visa, taught hands-on lessons of adaptation that erased common fears of the unknown by simple knowledge. Poppycock!

Mexico intrigued us!

La Pinta, Mexico, and The CAT

Sea of Cortez, Baja Pennisula, Mexico

The Sea in Moonlight

Charted Course

On the edge of the sea the moon's rising.
Diamonds strewn long the path of its beams.
Takes your breath! It's a magical moment.
Once again Mexico shares its dreams.
Choice of sea life has let us see wonders
that could never be found in a book.
Sea lure mixed with enchantments of nature,
treasures found on the course that we took.
There's a thousand or so miles of shoreline…
been a home to a handful of us.
We're the least in this Mexican homeland,
but they've shared it and been generous.
Family ties rule with natural acceptance.
Gives a pride 'mongst the rich and the poor.
As we're charmed by the deeds of their children,
we know basic beliefs form the core.
No questions asked why we've stopped here to harbor
and build boats for our family's abode.
Our paths crossed and we know though we're strangers;
life is planned from above for us both.
There's a pride in the fact that we're living
close to life's charted course, bound, yet free.
Salty dogs claim this map that was drawn; for
you and me and all mates love the sea!

No one enjoys rats because they're pests and we have to put up with them no matter what slice of earth is chosen for harbor. We ran into this species again thousands of miles from Alaska.

Rup and the boys provided some financial help to a group of land owners who were in danger of losing their property. It wasn't enough for one sour grape.

Yellow "Cat" in the Oyster farm

Sé Vendé/For Sail

Were they aware the role they played…
their lines rehearsed with flair;
or did they act as oft the case
without a thought or care?
Was there concern on why we came
or what we were about?
Each heart still owes itself account
for reasons we pulled out.
Desire instilled to pay each tax
came from an empty purse.
All gifts bestowed…each held in charge
to bless or else to curse.
The life we chose to live off land
is not our first concern
but more important is to hear
and give when it's our turn.
We came in peace…not to offend,
to build, share and abide..
till we felt tugged or pulled on by
the Master of the tide.
We'll take our boats…belongings too,
and leave without a fuss,
but often recollect how some
bad apples damaged us.

Parents don't alphabetically reminisce about their children or brag about them according to age. Good thing, because Bart is likely to pop up in any conversation, anywhere, without proper introduction. He's son number four and child six. Besides being a bike-nut early in life, like his dad, he also joined the Navy, but was an Airdale instead of a Seaman (GMSN).

Bart in the Navy, 1990, San Diego, California

When he finished his hitch, he headed for the Border, found his María, said, "We do," moved her on a boat and...started chartering.

Today, they have two children: Lillian Maria and Bart, Jr.

Bart, Jr. and Lillian at home on Catamaran, Sea of Cortez, Mexico

Bart and Maria, today, San Jorge, Mexico

Bart/Copy Cat

As a young child he prayed for a cycle,
didn't matter what size or what brand.
S'pose his Aunt B felt she was his angel
and delivered one...biggest on hand!
In the Navy he still dreamed of cycles,
not the three, but the two-legged kind.
Just a bike with a little more power
than his tricycle back down the line.
While a teen, his dad told him to first learn
each maneuver at lowest of speed.
Makes a safer more sure way to handle
any skill that a biker might need.
There's a smile ear to ear as he's living
in the Sea of Cortez on his Cat
with his wife plus a hound. Yes, a trike for
transportation that fits where they're at!

Painters dab from their palette.
God reaches up his sleeve.
Paintings by man are often priceless.
His aren't for sale;
but if patient we may
view another tomorrow.

Sunset over the Sea of Cortez, Mexico

The Painter

The golden lining on earth's edge

compares to fiery ambers

of wine that's stirred with cherry reds

poured down from sky's glass chambers.

The ruffled clouds above are spread

like velvet painted quilt tops

in glossy skeins of bright orange thread

and marbled works of spilled drops.

This gives the ocean mirrored sheen

reflecting colored copies…

all life stands still on glass lined seas

with waves no longer choppy.

Take one last drink of life's fine art

before day's close and sun's sank.

Be drunken just like me from awe.

And we think we can Still Paint?

Mexico has a special way of dealing with the unruly actions of some of the college kids that bombard this humble fishing village of Rocky Point during their Spring Break from the U.S.A.

Spring Break/U.S.A.

We've taken leave to Mexico
to live a life of ease.
We'll show these Mexicans just how
us gringos joke and tease.
We've brought our drink but eat their food
and dance with all their youth,
and tear up half the side of town
as we sip mixed vermouth.
Let's blaze the trail on back to light
our fireworks on the beach,
and, if time, dodge the little dogs
that wander by in reach.
We've raised all kinds of hell down here
and swindled all the poor,
while walking streets like kings and queens
cause we're just here on tour.
Oh, no! We never planned for this.
What's wrong? Could be a binge.
Quick! Point the way to baños, please…
it's Montezum's revenge!!!

Time out to walk the dog and our little grandson of two years. Let's learn a few lessons of desert survival. Chapo is the first born son of Rett and Cristina.

Their children are: Rett Rance, Jr. (Chapo), Grady (Pavy), and Peggy Sofía

Rett and Cristina

Rett, Jr. "Chapo"
Grady "Pavy"
Peggy Sofía

Below:
Dutch

Chapo and Dutch

Let's go down the beach and have a somersault or two;
squish the sandy mud up through our toes;
run the dog until his tongue has turned from red to blue;
chase the tide back out to see it flow.
Check the different shells the last storm left us for surprise;
splash along the shore until we're tired;
watch the blue horizon with few clouds up in the skies;
laugh at DUTCH cuz he's so doggone wired!
Skip-ty-doo across the crusted sand dunes left to dry;
see the birds go flitting off from shore.
Then you'll somersault once more and back to camp we'll fly,
wond'ring what tomorrow has in store.
Don't you walk by bushes when you can't see 'round them well,
there may be a rattlesnake or two!
Scorpions will hide in sand disguised so you can't tell.
They live in this Desert just like you.

The knot-ical course knot always points to seaward adventure. Nor do gunnels, masts and iron bark have to be the make-up of a flotilla's structure.

On the shore of Cortez, landlocked

Knot to forget the ultimate cure while "ship-ahoy" remains adrift: a sense of humor is a must for roughnecks locked out from their kind.

Our escape, someday! LOBO DEL MAR!

The sign on the refrigerator & Bunny Bee, Bar Harbor, Alaska

Temporarily Landlocked

We're not the type to justify the nonsense deeds we do
but after we had lived aboard, Rup, had me write a few.
We stuck them on the fridge…they read to somewhat this degree:
"If God intended us to live on land, how come the sea?"
The conversations this aroused with friends and guests alike
would always bring a snide remark or ribbing all in stride.
Much more than once our friends would say, "I'd love to live this life,"
and in the second breath would add, "but can't convince the wife."
We knew we'd found our niche in life that fit us like a glove,
and though t'was not a style for all, sure soothed nomadic love.
Now here we sit in landlock working on our next abode,
while pushing snakes and lizards out to build on our new boat.
This land lub life we're forced to live in R.V.s, one step down,
has taken quite a toll on Rup but won't take lying down!
As over near the wind shield there's a message he's appealed:
"If we were meant to stay one place, then why'd He give us wheels?"

As our four boats convoyed through the North Passage, unlike Rup, I had never been out of sight of land. But suspense filled with a certain wild expectation kept these fears submerged. To say we were hopelessly committed to the sea is an **understatement.**

When we completed our crossing of the Queen Charlotte Sound in Canada a half day later, we eagerly dropped anchor in a seemingly untouched, mind-unboggling refuge…Safety Cove. In this same light, the desert, sea and Mexico were now feeling like this same security blanket…just a tad warmer.

SEA WOLF,
San Juan Island,
Washington

SEA WOLF

Safety Cove

So you think this tug-of-war belongs to solomente, you?
Across the land you'll learn it's dealt with seven thousand too.
You're anchored fast and tied to life that's somehow lost its savor.
How can a man that's worth his salt support this waste forever?
The urge to shake yourself and fight this sleep that robs your goal,
is almost like a last call plea to wake up…take control!
Ideals are swapped for idols to be victimized at all.
Be proud you drew some lines back then, that's why you hear this call.
It isn't everyone who'll hear it, peculiar you should feel.
For most have slipped into a trance subjected by its will.
Be strong, have faith, act like a man, for there's a goal to claim.
I trust aft each life's struggle you'll find a haven of rest again.
We've found our cove of safety now and for a time we'll be
content…refreshed and happy in this desert near the sea.

Near the Columbia River, Rup was working as a millwright, welder. It was here that he fell eight feet and this accident would be the culprit that ended his welding career. After spending six months in the Seattle Rehabilitation Center, his doctors advised him to hang up his 'bonnet' and begin a pain management program. Rup has never been plan-free, or now, pain-free. Unwilling to be unproductive, his next creation was rigging a portable gadget over his bed to tie knots when that lower back turned monstrous. His macramé style is unique as he uses a sawed-off toothbrush with a slit slashed in it…ties a rubber band through the bottom.. affixes it to his belt loop and gets started. Belts, purses, shave kits, sea bags, hammocks, horse bridles… family and friends all share a piece of his works of art.

Rup on the farm in Texas, doing some fancy knot tying

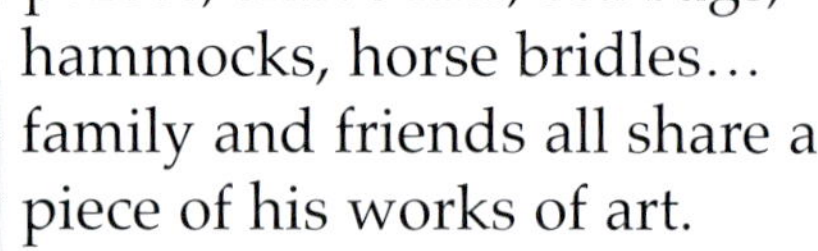

Sea-Borne Blues

Proper training's not the answer to recapture transpired years
of a family man who gets those sea-borne blues,
but someone who lives it with him holds his repertoire endeared,
and her secret's writing epics that are true.
Waking's moment dawned and with it flooding in with tales gone by
were our voyages to sea…outlined from shore.
Beached, encamped along the edges, time for hands on land to write
and to take a look at yesterdays aboard.
Spanish setting is my table on this desert dwelling lot
where we rest from building boats each night afar.
Thousand days gone by flow smoothly as the ink soaks up each thought
in our hacienda underneath the stars.
Turning pages in this family's lore, rereading prose rehearsed,
taking history notes regardless how I feel;
intellect proves not a 'must' here with this poet's rhyming verse,
for I'm looking back rewriting life that's real.
Dreamer, schemer, he's my subject, for without him where am I?
His affluence keeps me jotting inside out.
From the place he stands there's mountains and the ocean's always nigh…
it's apparent what his dreamin's been about!

There is one custom that Mexico has that we've always eyed and envied. Lucky that we now share birthdays so we can officially adopt it. The Piñata hangs there with little niños in mind but is confiscated by the teenagers who force the younger ones to walk the plank of piracy until its fate is spilled to the children's delight.

Party time,
San Jorge, Mexico
Chapo & Pavy

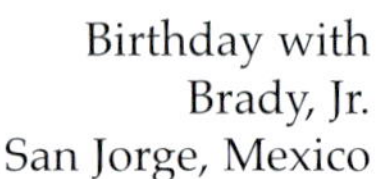

Birthday with
Brady, Jr.
San Jorge, Mexico

Piñata's Perch

Hanging there between two poles adorned for party-fest,
a bright Piñata stuffed with candy chaperones the guests.
The robbery of our kids' old masts from boats beached for repair
has been uplifting for the host with birds eye view from there.
The courtyard fills with friends and family for the birthday fun,
with kin extended and expanding, parties come each month.
A popped balloon from too much sun alarms one unaware.
His dignified and strained composure chuckles off the scare.
Soon, volleyball takes on the crowd of youngsters...oldsters too
on west side of the compound holding court for friendly feuds.
Throughout the day the native tongue is mixed with gringo drawl.
Interpretation's not that tough as Span-glish saves us all.
At last the children gather round with hopes the doll is full,
as teasing teens begin to blind fold each of them for duel.
The laughter heard across the desert as the candy spills…
we owe to each Piñata when its point of view's revealed.

SEA WOLF speaks Spanish — LOBO DEL MAR

Always fond of the logo, SEA WOLF, it doesn't surprise us to see it once again appear in our boat lineage. With a few strokes of the brush we'll have it speaking Español before the paint dries:

LOBO DEL MAR.

Lobo

Lean and mean the wolf portrayed…
cubs nestled in the den.
"Vermin of the plains," said they..
young pups obey its whims.
Savage tactics rule its day…
domesticated vows.
Vicious while it hunts the prey…
yet mates for life with spouse.
Quite often its the victim.
Indifferent, men proceed.
A wink of sleep won't slip them
to rob wolf's basic creed.
The rangy pelt-like donor
escapes so it might eat.
Although still stands a loner,
the lair brings brief retreat.
A lonesome hearted wonder
proved prowess from its birth
with grit protects its thunder..
this lone wolf of the earth.
Still wild unbroken fury
will drive this hungered beast,
till one day, God's Grand Jury
acquits… its struggles cease.
With pride we chose our logo
reputed by each scar.
Out on the ocean men know
our boat…LOBO DEL MAR.

At this writing we weren't pleased with the actions of a few of our kids. This was one of those depressed times that we dreaded leaving for Texas until things were straightened out...but we had to go. Anyone who has raised a family has at one time or other experienced these feelings of hopelessness.

Esperanza is a beautiful Spanish word
meaning "hope."

Esperanza

The road that leads us to the States still reads our deepest thoughts,
and offers its soft shoulder when we have to go distraught.
Each signpost marking exit as we leave Old Mexico,
reluctantly waves "adios" as we don't much want to go.
Soon, one-track minded traffic shifts to let us integrate.
Each car rolls' long and we're permitted on the Interstate.
Emotions fill our minds as we approach the trucks ahead;
with disappointments mounting as we pass…still nothing's said.
Our work and plans required a little more than sweat and tears.
Compassion for each other would have kept those duties clear.
We convoy through the night before most truckers stop to sleep
and see the writing on the wall this family fails to heed.
A still small voice tugs at the wheel as freeway flows dispense.
The flow that most go with is what we've warned the most against.
While high beams chart the path up front and darkness combats dawn…
God's tender mercies curb woe…esperanza moves us on.
These highway hurts now dissipate, we sense we're not alone
for as each star is tucked in bed, like them, we'll make it home.

We had just crossed the Line returning from Texas and with our usual home again sigh, made our way through the still-busy streets of Sonoyta as night fell…Mexico style!

Reaching the outskirts and heading out across the desert, I glanced over at Rup and felt his thoughts: "Just ninety 'klicks' to go and we'll be at the water's edge and the smell of salt." Fumbling for a pen, uncrumpling a page, I began scribbling by the light of the moon.

Carrol, Rup & Dutch

Harbor of Rocky Point, Mexico, and La Pinta

Sea Mates

Within these walls a man's life story
has forced these hands to tell his tale.
Records kept in memories store house,
drawn again from mind's deep well.
Shipwrecked from a life disastrous
'till the tide turned him around.
Finding refuge in deep water
was the new life he had found.
Foaming as the ocean raged wild,
kept him closer to his knees.
Safer now, although scoffed crazy,
this is where he made his peace.
Lofty ones so often mocking
how this man could seem at ease,
but another Friend upholds him
as He, too, once roamed the seas.

An education is essential, but it doesn't all have to take place in a classroom. Some lessons in life have to be learned with hard knocks.

My sister, Billie, from **Rupert**, Idaho, waiting in Prince **Rupert**, Canada to visit **Rupert** in Alaska!

Learning and Returning

Uprooting was tradition when our heels got dug-in tight.
Another job or venture always sprung up overnight.
Mar'time families learn to chart their field trips 'long the trail
of sea's historic school ground with aquatic show and tell.
Vacation doesn't bring a halt to lessons or to tests…
geography aboard's a daily challenge at its best.
Though seat of learning's prompted ' master art to stay alive,
psychology's abandoned..shunned entirely to survive!
Soon graduation from the sea through portals pomp-de-frills,
makes circumstance look passable to greener pasture thrills.
Adventure's not against the grain with parents true to self.
So apron strings are snipped as one by one each child takes sail.
Misfit these rovers come home fed up, they'll breathe salty air,
"Dad, get us back on board a boat, a jungle lurks out there!"

The boys finally got their go ahead so are busy working on our property and building houses along the shore of San Jorge for gringos. Still, life gets tedious when families bicker.

Rup "crowing" about his FM-3, which he earned long before the boys earned theirs

Roughing it in the desert sand

Rebel on guard at San Jorge, Mexico (Chapo's Jack Russel)

Harold

Eagles on Guard

On two acres in a strange land in the midst of sage and sand,
we are living in our campers, buses, tents, boats, R.V….vans.
From the early morn till sunset work goes on and on it seems,
on this little plot of heaven where each hopes to build his dream.
Learning patience takes more muscle than does actual brawns for stout
and our foe is just the mirror that returns a look of doubt.
In this God-forsaken desert feuds stand toe to toe to seize.
Those who've sold out are the victors…finding peace with God's the key.
Watch the eagle with sharp talons pluck the snake from its pursuit,
as the miner guards his gold mine leading villains from the loot.
Though we're often plagued by hear-say and in straits the Forces tease,
still can't help but feel protected as we build boats by this Sea.
While the Emblem shields the natural for us spread with foreign wings,
some Great Speckled Bird from heaven helps to keep that inward thing.

June is the month that ends like the beginning of the end. The gringos dissipate, so too, the tourist trade… as does our charter business. Gathering up "mucho" fortitude we try to make it through the next two and a half unbearable months. We've finally survived three summers here but stopping short of the border might prove disastrous.

As night cools the desert…all is forgiven.

The fence being built around our 2.2 acres...one block at a time

Brent with two rattlesnakes hanging on a rake...they were caught at the doorstep

Desert Home

Block by block the fence goes upward…keeping varmints out?
Built perhaps to keep us in our place.
Compass 'round the outskirts prairie dogs like pygmies scout,
watchful as they play close to their base.
Clouds are scarce so wind's hot breath blows cross the desert floor.
Cotton tails pursue the brush to hide.
Safety comes when caution's heeded near the serpent's door;
whether fleeting's safe…they must decide.
Dusk will offer shades of mercy with the even tide,
bringing halt to labor on this site;
dip its finger in the Sea for cooling brows' delight,
waking meanwhile creatures of the night.
Darkness muffles sounds of hoot owls gliding to their prey;
ceases birds from singing until dawn.
Stillness broken as the coyotes howl not far away…
yippin' puppies blazing trails they're on.
Once again this sun baked land awakes as coffee brews…
ushered in with warmth of day break cheer.
Birds strike up their melodies, while we sip down these views.
Desert happens! Aren't you glad you're here?

Looking back, there has never been any personal possession that Rup hasn't modified, improvised or changed. If so, the number's few. The change was most always an improvement…most always.

#1. Beautiful motorhome = 33′

#2. Nice looking van = 19′

Objective: Slice and dice until #1 fits under #2.

Reality: Rup and the boys really trashed my van!!!

Our RV before the trashing!

The van transformed.

After.....

Beastly Beauty

We swapped our boat in Ketchikan and when the trade was done
an R.V. used for payment greeted us.
We found a spot in Mexico where we could soak up sun…
the place our motor home would bite the dust.
The task of building boats was not a major feat, I guess,
though six times two makes twelve hulls with their keels.
Our man-in-charge decided that the Dodge could use finesse,
so this is when the R.V. lost its wheels.
They dropped the under carriage of this Spanish home discussed
before the head-of-house could change his mind
and put the entire chassis, plus the engine and its stuff,
right underneath our van to get aligned.
A sight to see, a stretch van that's been dwarfed…somewhat a shame!
'Bout six feet on each end was hanging out.
But when the boys had cut it back to fit the size of frame,
a giant now stood and with it came their shouts!
"Come see this beauty, mom! It has to be a work of art!"
Well, maybe! If I had the eyes of men!
But there it stood a brut on wheels…and me without my car
so, take it fellars, it's your BEAST to tend!!

The mixed emotions of the desert have been sun pleasure with sun drear; an oasis because of an ocean, desert, mountain mixture. The minimal shade and maximum rays gives Old Sol a stroke of luck with our nerves and webbed-feet.

Beached in San Jorge, Mexico

Fish Out of Water

There's a pathway in the desert that leads down to open sea
with a tide land that runs dry almost a mile.
In this Sonora Desert hot land camped along the shore-side lee,
we hold hands with Mother Nature in the wild.
On the banks of this flat dry land sets a Cat, each hull of white.
Anchored out a short hop further are two more.
Built to scale, but somewhat shorter, both are held in sheer delight
as the giant that's being built along the shore.
In the distance we're protected by the mountains that transpose
to a different hue…depends on time of day.
Although aged and weather beaten, they seem wise with telltale throes,
as the handwork part of nature on display.
We're the guest of honor in this desert of Sonoran gems,
more than privileged to be transfixed by its view;
with a front row seat to scope the sunrise as each day begins,
and the same seat's offered us at sunset too.
So our stay in Mexico has been a mixed emotion treat,
as the desert by the sea keeps us alive.
We've worked hard to get these Cats built and move on them when complete;
as a fish when out of water…starts to die!

Sea of Cortez, Mexico

Just a little time spent on wondering about the deeds done in our lifetime. Time out!

Fairbanks, Alaska

Masterpiece

Campfires stimulate the senses of our inner thoughts.
Somewhere out there One has answers to all questions sought.
Sitting by the fireside musing how great men excel
and just where their knowledge comes from, which man do we hail?
Swift and silent comes suggestions while they dream in beds.
Isn't that like Old Man wisdom, playing with men's heads?
Shipwrights build each ship to handle gale-forced storms and seas,
while the canvas takes new meaning on the artists' knees.
Spoken into minds of craftsmen comes a thought inspired,
then the gifteds' wheels start spinning till result's acquired.
Who will rightly claim the fame each masterpiece has wrought;
take full credit for production; wasn't it a thought?
True, the masterminds' ingenious shines as laurels ought.
Credence goes, though, one step higher, where all men are taught.
If awards are never granted for this family's role,
one thing life on sea has taught us, God is in control!

We have to pay tribute and a few pages to our nine dogs. They each hold two places of value?

#1 **Worthless** and #2 ***Priceless***

Good thing we've never had to barter with kid versus dog—good luck and have a nice life—kid! We would introduce them, properly but these "priceless" mongrels are at present, busy protecting us from the sea gulls along the shore and the shy, but curious prairie dogs that sneak peeks, hourly. Wonder why these turbulent rovers steer clear of the beehive at the end of the compound?

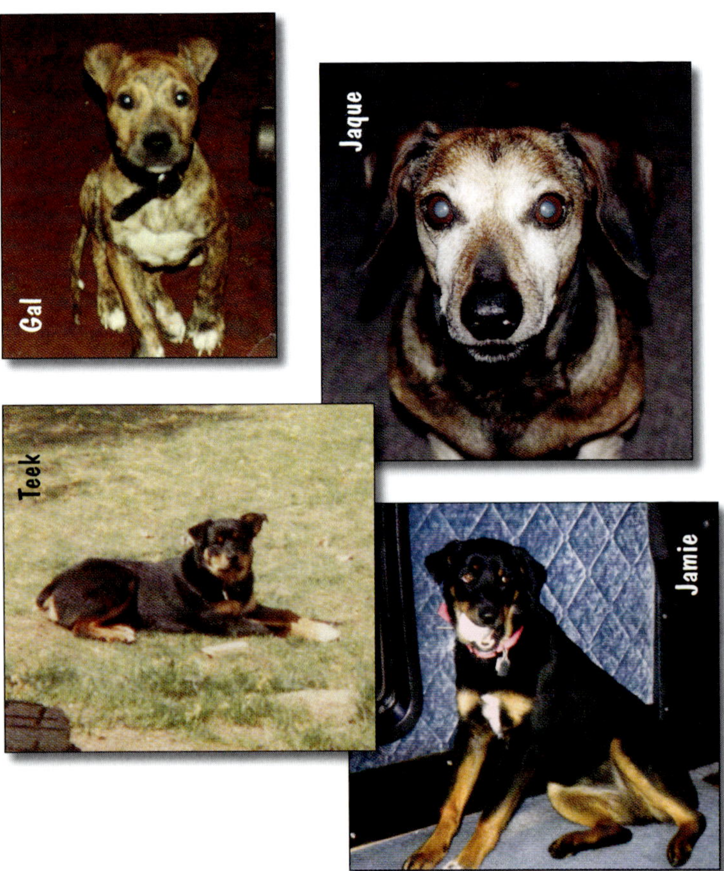

Our Dogs

GAL (Rett's)

Born his brindle bound for Baja
via Northern Lights for starts,
Terrier/Bull though aged from 'pit' stops
GAL still reigns as Queen of Hearts!

JAQUE (Bridget's)

There's a long-g wheel base out digging.
He's a weener wound-up tight.
As he digs his way to 'China'
in the backyard, JAQUE'S a sight!

TEEK (Brent's)

Black and Tan, a jumping jack
an agile deer at play,
this Heeler/Rott, with brut-force, guards.
TEEK's master of the day.

JAMIE (Ruppy's)

Proud pedigree dons Heeler/Rott;
she struts with poise and charm.
Luxuriant coat; face sweet and slim,
our JAMIE'S one sleek 'marm.'

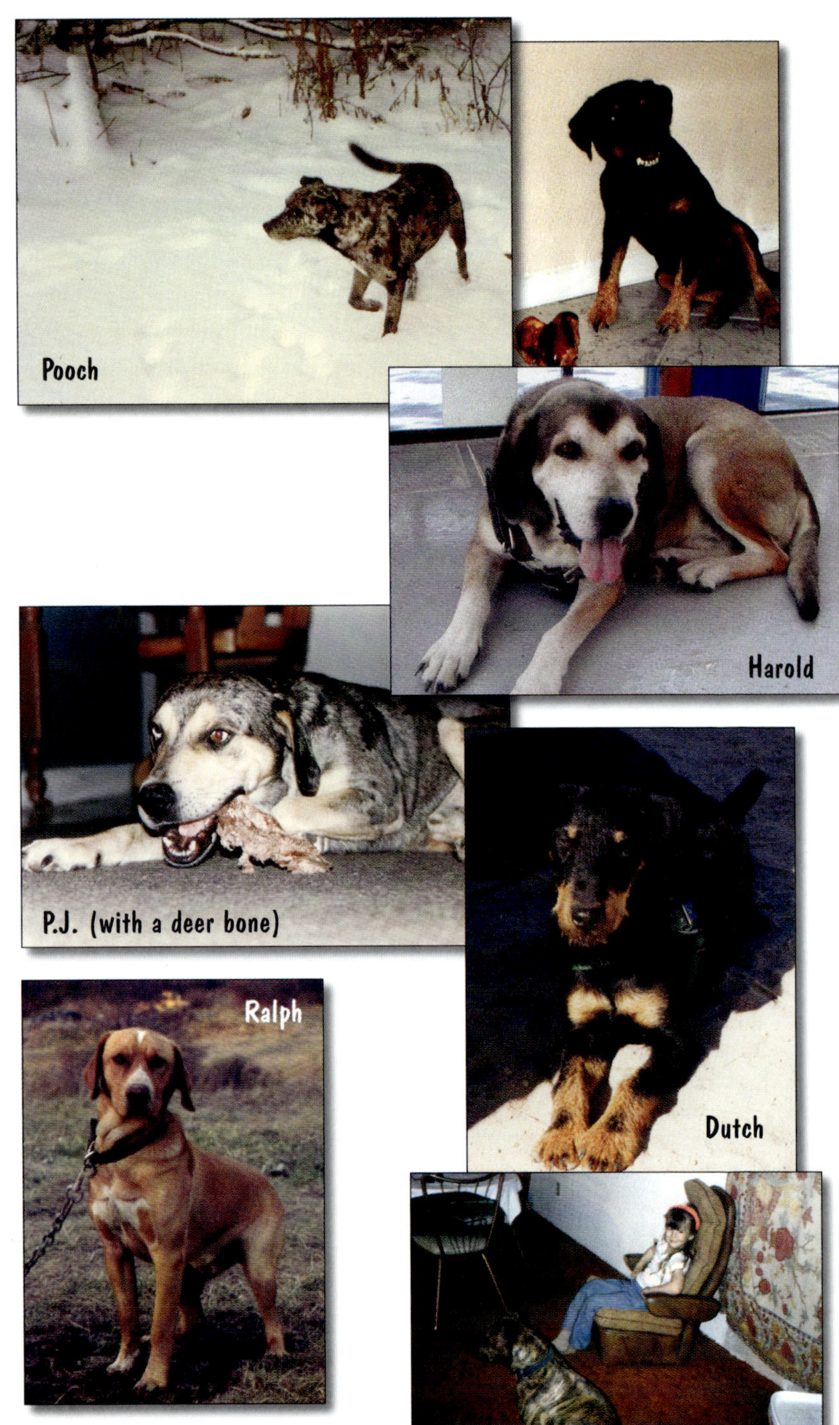
Pooch
Harold
P.J. (with a deer bone)
Ralph
Dutch

Our Dogs (Continued)

POOCH (Brady's)

POOCH, a timid, bashful Pit
bred Heeler for disguise.
With stealth-like moves he stalks his foe;
a spotted-coat SURPRISE!

HAROLD (Bart's)

In this Hound-dog's world today
new-learned tricks, with treats abound.
Handsome mug this masked-face shows us,
HAROLD'S one smart and well-trained Hound.

P. J. (Buck's)

P.J., with long ears, alert,
takes heed to far-off calls;
squint-eyed slipping past his lord
bounds off to have a ball!!

DUTCH (Rupert's)

Obnoxious DUTCH, a beastly Jag
with savage tactics plays
without reverse and marches forth
to hunt his helpless prey!

RALPH (Brandy's)

Brown-eyed puppy, boasts this Pit
marked with show-dog style and pride.
Gold Retriever, coat's the same,
RALPH can turn in his own hide.

One of the old fashioned theories we borrowed to raise the family with was, “one has, all has.” Not a hard-fast rule, just general.

Responses ranged from: “Seems to work,” to “Outdated!” But, by jove, it works!

Bunny Bee was up in North Pole—chasing reindeer? On the contrary. She was waiting tables at the “Moose’s Tooth.” But her curiosity was working over-time, so she headed South to look for a tiny baby “rabbit,” who was running ‘round loose.

Brent y Léo’s familia:

Bunny Luz

Brent Jr.

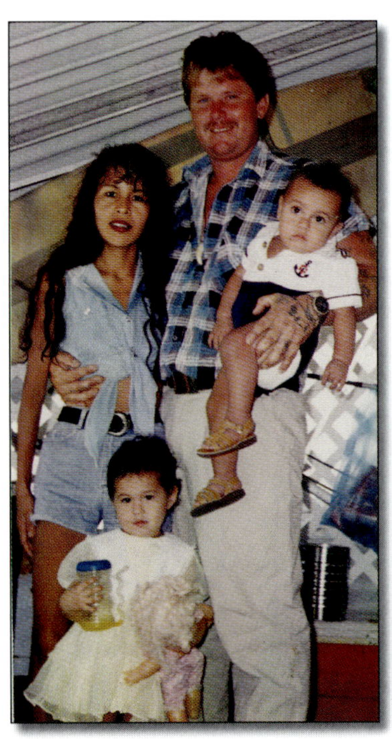

La Conéja

The caribou that roam the Northern slopes on chilly nights,
(Alaska's nights are usually six months long)
have shared their frozen tundra with a Bee near Northern Lights,
but Bunny chucked it all and then was gone.
The family had her boat afloat, so this could change her world.
The Cortez Sea is famous for this style.
She learned she was an Aunt, again, a 'bouncing, bubbly girl,'
her name-sake, so it could be worth her while.
Now down below the U.S., Rocky Point held something 'dear.'
Border-crossing, Bunny, found it so.
As there within the desert by the shore she saw it clear,
another Bunny 'Luz' in Mexico.

This summer's heat is not for whimps! Rup and I are out of here!

Seriously, I do believe we would be able to stay for the duration if the man-who-doesn't-always-listen would have donned his helmet during a bike trip through Arizona's Desert the year before last, fouling his temperature gauge.

Brady on his classical and Bart belting out ballad tunes have entertainment drifting from dwelling to dwelling on a moon-lit stage that couldn't be any more magnifico, anywhere.

Brady & Bart,
San Jorge,
Mexico

Heavenly Hideaway

This habitat, on fire by day, demands a stifled breeze
for summer's sun rules like some 'solstice king.'
But hidden is our hideaway that's hushed as hopes appease
the span of land transposed when nighttime sings.
The square on which we've 'pitched our tents' begins to cool, a bit,
and slowly each one gathers to his own.
The sheets are turned-down for the night in everybody's slip,
while dappled shades of twilight hugs each home.
"Flamenco" comes alive, as does the Milky Way, tonight,
when tones drift from a boat in classic runs.
In solitude we share again Creation's star-flung lights,
and feel the 'magic' of each note that's strummed.
The stillness from our dwellings as we listen in the quiet
to gypsy-like ensembles of his strings;
all find it hard believing that the music of this night
is rhythm coming from one lonely being.
A bonfire in the distance, smolders low with mixed debris
while yet another son recites in song.
We've made it through another day, his melody agrees,
with trust the family's plan soon comes along.
Reclined upon our boat, you watch the last few embers pale.
We both hear households, one by one, retire.
Tomorrow's strength attained; out there somewhere a coyote wails,
as sleep puts out our Spanish campsite fire.

In reality, there's possibly much gold left in the mountains surrounding the sea. As there's signs of old abandoned mines up 'thar.'

Rup's first desert encounter was before school-age in Rainbow Valley, Arizona. He and his dog roamed the sweet potato fields which his dad irrigated, almost hidden, in the middle of this desert.

My dad put us on a train in Georgia after WWII, and we eventually ended up in Twin Falls. This Magic Valley, in Idaho, appeared as a field snatched from the sagebrush, with the desert lurching outside this spud-land to retrieve. But now, here we both are sharing a new Desert, a gem of Sonora, by the beautiful CORTEZ of Mexico!

Bird Island, favored diving spot in the Sea of Cortez, Mexico

A view of the mountains and our desert "Retreat"

Gem in the Rough

Gazing out beyond this compound past our desert camp;
watching morn's unveiling calm a mystic, dim-lit lamp.
Day springs up the backside part of far-off mountain range,
casting shades and shadows dark which form a sketch so strange.
Silhouettes on top the mount like sleepy towns at dawn.
Wonder why this would astound, this ridge no life lives on?
Clouds prepare their hoax outlined on sunrise all in play,
just before they fall behind the skies to guard the day.
Multitudes of morning dreams, with never one the same,
out here in the desert, scenes excel the Hall of Fame.
Seems a land deserted, face-less, by the salty sea.
Beauty in this barren waste excites the likes of me.
Unrevealed, except to few, this diamond in the rough;.
kept concealed on purpose to protect its finer stuff.

Spirited, Spartan-like splendor!

It was my turn to awaken from sound sleep, hear the distant surf, gaze upward to question an unknown constellation (Two in the early morning is not my usual astronomy moment!) and toss the urge-to-wander thought around and around while ignoring the virtues of patience.

Sunset over the Sea of Cortez, Mexico

Carrol...dreaming

Fuego De Gitana

Tonight the offshore breezes leave a message meant for me.
A path across the moonlit way awaits my company.
The cool caressing wind awakes this gypsy fire again,
and gently fans the flame that flickers from a depth within.
Reaching for the door that's closed until the proper time;
watching through the porthole, patience seems a pain of mine.
Reminiscing stirs the embers. Warmed, we'll both soon say,
"Adios, vaya con Dios," getting underway.

LOBO DEL MAR Charters, our business name on the compound and charter service, of course. The only boat operating in the beginning was the 38 foot "Cat" belonging to Bart and Maria. Their baby girl, Lillian, was a delight to all, and correctly nicknamed "Willie Bug." But the brawniness that had to be used by the LOBO's crew to "ferry" the clients in and out was just as noteworthy as the cruise.

Gringo Wagon, San Jorge, Mexico

Our Yellow Sailboat

Bird Island, with its Pelicans, Sea Lions & Seals

Holding Down the Fort

On its way across the water, churns astern wee rippled wake,
scoots a little yellow sailboat—double hulls for comfort's sake.
With the lad who's dubbed "El Captain" works his wife
(she's First Mate, too);
but their "Willie Bug's" the highlight, main attraction of the crew.
Each excursion brings much pleasure to all clients brought on board,
still, Bird Island's destination gives a 'seal'-approved reward.
Birds and seals invade this island (mixed aroma fills the air)
in the middle of the ocean far and free from anywhere.
But behind each cruise and charter is the crew who stay ashore;
some to hustle up more business, some to muscle guests aboard.
As we share our sea-life treasures on the chartered boat resort
we've some pirates beached, but hearty, holding-down the LOBO's fort.

The laws in our society are so designed to make it against the law to be poor.

Sonoran Desert & Mountains

Untainted Desert

The desert is a thirsty land that can't distract Old Sol
from drinking most the hidden cache of water for its fold.
The creatures, with each plant, form pacts to play the waiting game
until their thirst has been revived with drops of saving rain.
It's just the course of nature, not against the rules of life
to deal with drought and famine in the desert to survive.
The same holds true for families, here, that do the best they can.
It's not against the law to be a poor man in this land.
But midst this people, poor and rich they still untainted stay,
for each can claim the simplest art of living for each day.
The coyotes, soon, will quench their thirst; the plants will start to mend,
and folks will sigh because they see the desert bloom again.

After purchasing a piece of Mexico, we divided a portion of it into individual family lots, and the remaining part into R.V. space rentals, boat construction and storage.

Library looking forward

The three catamarans had been hauled out for seasonal repair, but the fourth one was the boat that had my interest. We didn't know if it could swim as it hadn't had its keels wet. It's huge, it's lovely, but it's beached!

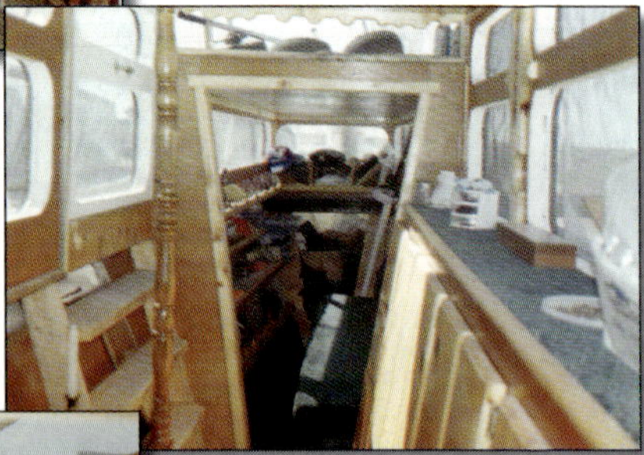

Inside
Our "Cat"

"Rec" room,
looking aft

One Thing at a Time

Too many months have slipped away with projects left and right,
and still our boat keeps sitting there without a sign of life.
We both keep staring at each hull, then sneak a peek inside.
A glimmer flashes gleefully we each try hard to hide.
The first thought 'aired' without debate is fix a day-bed so
that maybe every now and then a nap when things get slow.
But somehow odds and ends have left the R.V., unaware,
and relocated in the boat as if intended there.
I've taken daily, just a few things, not to cause alarm,
and he, too, slips some undetected, 'course intends no harm.
Within a week we've both confessed as common sense assumes,
and now agree we'd best move on before there's no more room.

Rup with a Gringo Wagon,
San Jorge, Mexico

Only a beached sailor can hear that far-off call and feel like the most miserable human being on the face of this earth. I should know, I'm living with him!

Tide flats, San Jorge, Mexico

Homesick for La Vida Del Mar

Quickly, how the time is fleeting shown by sand-signs in the dial,
Spanish-speaking Mexico has pampered us in desert style.
Now, so anxiously awaiting for the chance to go afar,
really homesick for 'la vida' once we lived upon del mar.
Western Desert of Sonora's coaxed us on by starlit nights,
making sure of our provision with its warmth from sunny skies.
Far-off's call; a voice enticing; audible to seamen ears,
and the squelch will not be hushed until that 'somewhere' comes in clear.
With the bottom paint quick-drying, and the last hatch fastened tight,
rolling in like waves uplifting launching day has come in sight.
Hope renewed and sojourn's ending. Shrouded is our bliss no more.
Soon, we'll answer journey's bidding when we leave this friendly shore.

Aye, He knew what was needed when the sunrise rose.

The stage is set with the distant mountain range touching the floor of this desert; desert nudges sea; sea goes on forever and ever in both directions.

The rich must feel so poor and the poor, so rich.

My father-in-law "went to bed with the chickens" and got up the same and together never missed a sunrise.

Red Road, Sunrise
Puna, Hawaii

Papa at Sunrise
inTexas

Sunrise

The panorama stage of lights
across the barren land
reflects the shadows of the dawn
in luminescent bands.
The setting for this daybreak film
in ever changing hue
would span the universe to air
its fine resplendent view.
This scene I chanced to waken to;
an early morning play,
and watched spell-bound for, oh so long,
to grasp its choice display.
There's one, I know, who'd never missed
the rising of the sun,
to watch its triumph of the night
as it had always done.
Nor can some ever share the sights
recorded in their hearts,
just as the man who paints still-life
can't capture this on charts.
I'll step up first to claim my guilt
for all the morns I've missed,
and find it sad because of dawns,
forever, been dismissed.

If there ever was a "moment" for soul-search, sunset qualifies. Last minute splendor accelerates the urgency of night fall's forte.

Should a sailor on shore get blue? These sailors do!

Sunsets over the Sea of Cortez, Mexico

Sunset

Red skies tonight's a sailor's delight
and fits our fancy, too,
the reddest, red in fire-brands of light
captured in sea-front view.
Just now the sun, far brighter than day,
slides down yon mountain-side,
with one last fling of fireworks in spray,
it settles down for night.
Along the shore, a hazy twilight
has cast its colors, pale
in shades so soft with tinges of night
and blues as swabbies' bells.
The close of day's one glorious eve
but ties our hearts in knots.
For as the sailor's tied to sea
our cord's no lesser taut.
The tide, in ebb, is leaving again
and we're left yearning so.
Amidst the dusk in shadowy blends
our souls keep crying, "Go!"
The edge of night tells after-glow lore
that leave us in a rut.
Though we're on shore, our living aboard's
one cord that can't be cut.

Moonlight over the North Pole, Alaska

Listen to my description of the moon and I'm obliged to listen to yours. And so it goes, never ending.

Pick a Spanish night; toss in the water's edge; dot it with shadow-like underbrush and faint shadings of hillsides; step into its circle. You're standing in the center of the universe. You've just been captured by "LUNA'S LUSTER."

Luna's Luster

Night's evening shades are pulled like curtains 'round our boat once more,
that's cradled in the desert here while dry-dock near the shore.
This dry-land's been our home away from home upon the sea
and entertained us nightly with small wonders up its sleeve.
A treasure chest discovered when the moon exposed its gold,
in contrast with each planet's silver stardust we behold.
Bright candles lit across the heavens from the Evening Star
all twinkling like a million fire-flies bringing warmth to dark.
With breath held tightly here on board to see this night unfold,
our captured gaze keeps taking in horizon's pot of gold.
Big golden moon still coming up until completely round,
and from the boat we see it on the edge of night aground.
Each utters Oh! and Ah! and Wow! as quietly as we dare--
I guess we feel our whispers might affect events out there.
The luster of moon's brilliant gold midst silvery, sparkling gleams
claims silence of a thousand worlds as backdrop for this scene.
Not one of us would say, "Enough!" and chase this eve away,
so, evening shades again are raised to start another day.

The overhauled pickups that were transformed into 'one' in SLEEPY's poem are/is the CHE-FORD spoken of in the following.

This hauling rig in its entirety was both pathetic and ingenious. That (only) half mile to the beach without proper equipment may as well have been to the moon. The boys put their 'all' into this last-ditch attempt to get their folks back onto good pasture.

Climbing that make-shift ladder to home, while turning to catch their approval inspired this poem, following, from the boy's point of view.

CHE-FORD

Bird Island Sanctuary, 14 miles from San Jorge and a favorite dive spot for the Dive School, welcomes 1000's of sea lions, pups, and as many birds.

Back to the Sea

It wasn't how the three rigs fared that caught us by surprise,
nor that the scaffolds built them weren't an architectural rise.
The trailer that was used so many times to transfer boats
was made from 'scratch' to haul each "Cat" from Texas on its float.
But now the 'little fellar' strained from cargo strapped to it.
A nightmare hung on either side—some dreamt-up freighters' fit.
Wee Datsun tied and slashed to stern from underneath, peered wrecked,
as seven beams of steel support yacht's sixty foot of deck.
The Chevy truck, (or was it Ford?), was power used for this quest,
but midget pickup steered from rear in case of S.O.S.
The wild-men who'd attempt this feat (geared so unorthodox,
plus try to move a craft this size) heads must be full of rocks.
With snail's pace speed towards seaside beach the caravan resumed,
as inch by inch, with six defeats, found 'half mile' almost doomed.
Contraptions are a work of art if they react as planned;
this project reaching shore reflects some wits in desert sand.
But shocking were two instant smiles returned from two years' roam;
we watched both scramble 'board this "Cat"— our dad and mom are home!

The tide is like God; it gives, it takes! No matter the situation, whether we come out the better for it, or the worse, we do acknowledge that the last word belongs to God. If it's bad news, we swallow very hard. If it turns out good, we make plans! Sometimes we may not understand. We do have to accept the out-come, and do our best with it.

The "five" boys spoken of in the poem following are:

Rett,

Brent,

Bart,

Brady and

Juan (He is Cristina and Leo's brother,
but we took him in as one of ours too,
several years ago. He has his lot on the
"Compound" also, and lives in his
Motor Home.)

Juan, Brady, Bart, Rett and Brent, today,
in the Harbor at Rocky Point, Mexico

High Stakes

The toolbox washed up on the beach used now for us a seat;
two weary mates sit licking wounds from last night's near defeat.
The thrill of yesterday is gone but now amidst the wreck
a wave of pride from years of toil is holding back regret.
We watch the five boys, agile, poised, use skills taught from their dawn,
with each son grabbing tasks at hand, the foe is met head-on.
Against the odds they fight the sea as fate laughs back in glee
and with a 'victory roll' it swamps each hull with surf's debris.
As night surrounds the campfire and the 'five,' exhausted, sigh;
they know they played their hands to max, but inward question, "Why?"
In private all five search their souls (each silent plea would trod),
unknown, they weave a cord of five-strands to the throne of God.
The wind is up and bringing with it floods of billowy waves.
Disaster's sure, both hulls awaiting for their watery graves.
But Wait! a change of orders from the realm of Utmost Power;
a treaty signed with wind and waves, "Be still through this dark hour!"
And with that, suction loosens grip and sets the 'prisoners' free;
the hulls leap forth with bull-like force and slide onto the sea!
What token to express our thanks could we as parents, boast?
Instead we've learned we must let go of what's not valued most.
We pray the stakes, you five, drove in will help abide your time
and be the first 'down-payment' on your mansion up the line.

"Once a sailor, always a sailor," is a tattooed truth that runs very deep in ocean-dipped veins. Waiting is much more difficult than running as we relearn this every day, here, building, sweating and waiting, waiting some more.

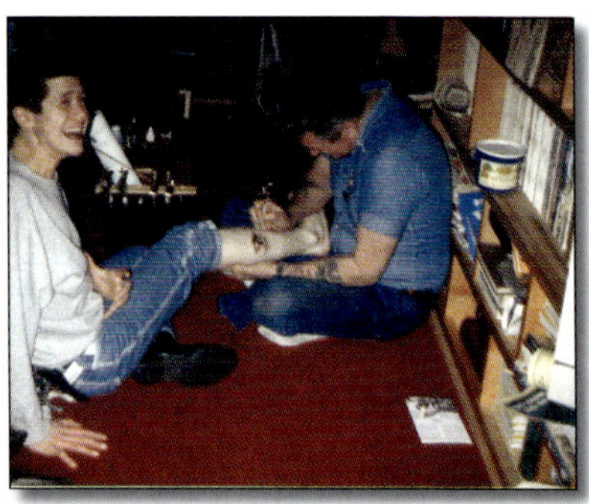
Brady & Rup practicing,
Bar Harbor, Alaska

Speaking of tattoos; when Rup bought a 'machine' a few years ago, he and Brady kept making 'dry' runs. When I finally discerned the gleam in their eyes, I made Rup promise that he would not dare try-out his "R-Teestic" skills on that kid until a few months of practice on an orange (the recommended procedure)! He promised! A few HOURS later, Brady was sporting an EAGLE!!

Now the whole family has at least one, somewhere. The boys would give each other some pretty noteworthy ones on rainy days in Ketchikan. Judging from the number displayed on their arms, it rained a lot!!!

Oh, and by the way, that one 'machine' turned into six machines with all the supporting equipment.

Rett, Brady,
Bucky and Brent...
sporting a few signs
of a "rainy day"

Desert Dream

Casting shadows on the sandy path that leads away from shore,
as the evening sun descends the Western stairs;
wond'ring what lies in the shade ahead, we both again implore,
will that pot of gold, this time, be waiting there?
Rainbow's promise never let us down—that vow has stood the test,
but a prayer for finer castles never ends,
so the wish of strong-holds fitting and in truth would suit us best
is a vessel built to harness wave and wind.
Picket fences aren't for everyone, as terra firma learns,
once a sailor sacrifices land for sea;
heaving anchor to while farewells fall, unheard, on salty stern
that's been swapped for someone's palace to be free.
Ocean waters, unknown silences, and white-capped broken crests
have appeal to untamed places in the soul;
often cutting deep and wide from one sea-venture to the next,
as exposure to these forces makes one whole.
Twilight threat'ning, now, the home-front, once again, as dusk draws near;
so the answer didn't come for us this day.
Desert dreams made in Old Mexico perhaps will soon appear
when our 'ship comes in' reality that way.

Casting away confidence and losing hope isn't healthy, so I deal with this guilt. Our boat mishap has left me reeling with multiple anxieties of doubt, depression and self pity.

But for me to watch Rup, a man who has truly loved his time of tides; his pride of every boat owned and the great privilege of operating each; knowing these dreams are now awash, I try hard to hold on for him, and wait...

Son of the Sea

Son of the Sea

Those islands in the distance, longed
for once, are just a haze
and out of reach, forever, as
horizons drift away.
Whatever waits beyond them, now,
must keep their secrets quiet
and batten down their expectations
dreamed of in the night.
Without direction or a plan
for hands which labored long,
this stout of heart seems limp and
calloused from a tide gone wrong.
What is this never-ending love
with ever-taunting fears,
that's challenged from the cradle and
contended through the years?
How can the feel of swells beneath
becalm a skipper's grief?
Would be the breath of life at sea
restores his firm belief!
Without a boat there is no hope
for seamen locked ashore;
a wild-man jailed without a key
could fare a good-sight more.
Contentions in the current's flood,
unseen won't let him be,
till fate has closed its gates and ebb
tide frees son of the sea.

While our turn-around trips continue (to check on mom) family trails have taken off in every direction... Hawaii, Alaska, and Old Mexico. San Jorge's project is needing financial help!

One or a few of the children designated to stay with "Granny" and maintain the small, 17-acre farm "Papa" left her in '92 is the family's chief priority.

We've never begrudged her wanting to stay near the memories of the one whom none of us in this lifetime will ever, nor could ever forget.

Mom "Granny" Buntin at 80 with Sam, Alaska

Bedspread "Granny" crocheted for me years ago

Our Granny

Her chair, reclined, has felt but half a friend to Gran these days,
mixed feelings from sweet memories since her children went away.
Those cool Hawaiian Trade Winds played unfair with all her dreams;
in trade they took her grandkids leaving miles of sea between.
True, studies of each photo makes her marvel how they've changed.
That doesn't stop her fretting that Alaska's out of range.
Oh, maybe there's a 'Northern Light" with fearsome polar bears
but worries, more, her family may get snowed-in way up there!
With little prayers said daily for the ones who've headed South;
so often she's regretting that the desert sand won out.
Yes, Mexico's held liable if those grand-sons ever whine,
as señoritas helped them waltz across the Texas line.
That rocking chair has held and helped a-many grand-child grow
and tracked-down loved ones born to roam cross sand and sea and snow.
As Granny frets but ponders round the few who've stayed behind,
we'll keep tabs on this TEXAN for she's lived a long, long time.

If one stands in the desert with one foot in the sea; aware of the salt; experienced voyages rescued from the deep; felt the calm before the storm; lived to sail another day; how can that one not write about waves and wind?

Winds and Waves

As the ocean swells with darkness
gloom and silence break in wails
howling, screeching, forcing seas on,
wind-ward overpowers the gales.
Like a serpent loose to run wild
winds have terrorized the waves.
Hope is lost to flee its clutches;
only chance is fight like braves.
Recklessly, the foe keeps pushing,
helplessly, the braves obey,
twisting, reeling, churning, smoking
while the night screams to betray.
Without mercy, time seems heartless.
Will salvation lose this fight?
Is this agonizing storm tossed
just to rob sea's peaceful plight?
Help at last! A soft breeze whispers,
while embracing sea from war,
calming waves with soothing ripples
as it gently hugs the shore.

This poem was written in two sessions. When Rup and I received videos from the children now living and working in Hawaii (Oahu and Hawaii, the big island), I was sold! Besides, mom was there with them, too. But I wanted to see it for myself, live. After jotting down a few thoughts, I laid them aside. Rup had seen Hawaii during his teens and someday wanted

Our Welcome-to-Hawaii gang consisted of Gretchen & Rachael (granddaughters), B.B. (daughter) and Sue (daughter-in-law). We came for 2 weeks & stayed for 5 months.

to return with his family and to all the other places he docked during his Navy hitch. Well, we'd had that privilege begin to take place when we tied our lines to Canada's wharf many years ago, then Alaska's, next Mexico's. Could

Hawaii possibly be added to this lifeline? Soon we left our unfinished boat behind, and still ground-tied to port (airport) that is, in Honolulu, Hawaii. Now, I'm eager and looking forward to the rest of those "ports." But first, I have a poem that's needing finished.

Been There!

When camera captures bits and pieces,
scenes of expertise unroll.
Far better, though, when naked eye sees
life and beauty it beholds.
To breathe and feel sights for ourselves is
what 'reel' dreaming's all about.
For pictures, although "worth a thousand
words," alive are more than clout.
Don't ever stop that cam's recording,
making imprints someday told.
Poetically, your mind is storing
thoughts your diary keeps in rolls.
Have staggered from the viewing room where
captivation had us pinned.
Now paradise has made us victims
of your Island's foliage sins.
Since staring at the films you'd sent us,
watching re-runs, 'fraid to budge;
we'd really rather be the first-hand,
"been there,done that" kind of judge.
Some take a book down from the mantle
finding, feeling, freedoms far.
But we felt better with a ticket.
So, "Aloha!" here we are!

As I'm sitting occasionally during a quiet time and observing where we are, where we've been, life; death; nature and see its beauty; penning a few thoughts seems inevitable.

The Admiral

We count the falling stars at night and watch Orion rise
but feel there's more than stardust where the oceans meet the skies.
To be aware of HIS domain, to sense what's still unknown;
indeed, this present universe seems but a stepping stone.
And—"Let there be a firmament," (in spite of disbelief),
was Heaven's birth the 'second day' and ordered by the Chief.
To scale HIS omnipresence where dominions cannot climb,
this treasure never measured in our finite state of mind.
Permission, now, to come aboard and view the plan, in part;
no longer time in timeless space, no eons there to chart.
With absolute celestial rule where stars are fixed for fame,
all planets circuit at HIS will; each sextant reading's vain.
We'll trust the Chief Commander's touch when storm clouds overwhelm,
to steer us past sea's perils with HIS presence at the helm.

When we first arrived on the Big Island of Hawaii, Rup took me on a bike ride down the RED ROAD! It was breathtaking, it was gorgeous, and it was my scariest ride to date.

Arriving home to the Thanem's (Lars, B.B., and children) regaining my balance and bearings, I knew that this Hawaiian King Kamehameha deserved an "ode to his road."

The Red Road in lower Puna, Hawaii

The King's Highway

Kamehameha's royal trail remains a traveled turf;
this kingly path, though, hides beneath the paved.
For while the 'locals' share the RED ROAD to their favored surf,
his foot print's swallowed up by modern ways.
Our novice presence on this road-way plagues all driving skills,
preoccupied as waves wash 'cross the bars.
Where land meets sea, our calm composure flees as visions' thrilled;
in nick of time, we dodge oncoming cars!
The bike now gains the upper-hand and cruises long the sea,
while mango and papaya groves exceed.
With twilight time from dawn till dusk from over-hanging trees,
those potholes lurk in stealth to check our speed.
We haven't reached the "breaking point" this Island favors most,
most Puna-ites prefer in place of school;
but 'catching waves' is safer, far, than driving down this road,
where 'catching fenders' seem the biker's rule.
We love this ocean's bluest, blue in hue that mocks the sky's;
the shore that grapples with the shoal and foam;
have understood the King who walked across this paradise,
as we should have, and left our bike at home!

The warmest feeling on earth is belonging, being a part of a group or a family. It may take years before some realize what group or slot they fit in. Meeting your family is not of chief importance, just knowing you're connected, somehow. It's not a vicious circle, actually, but rather very orderly. Those without purpose or place are those left spinning their wheels.

Grandsons Pavy, Trevor and Chapo enjoy a Hawaiian beach

Somewhere, Someday, Somehow

Time began and pulled into the gravity of life

a man stands in its circle, somewhere destined, and his wife.

One soul amongst a million others placed in moment's grasp;

like them, his days are numbered, also midst the circuit's path.

Devotion pre-bound in him not to win wars for the Prince;

indeed, through dedication to his King he's vowed defense.

Would be his lot on planet's sod to trade land for the sea;

with wander-lust built-in there'll someday be a family fleet.

Each to his own by solemn grant, and boundaries, too, decreed;

for grief of life comes when trespassing on ungotten deeds.

Surrounded by all mariner mates now stowed-away in time,

predestined, sea-girt, life ties his to ring-of voyager's line.

Antiquity seems tranquil somehow to this way-worn child,

whose thoughts derived near ocean's bank came from shore's ageless file.

Around this earth's worn past, to now, an ordered chart began;

each sailor comes full-circle as the Ancient, Old Man planned.

Ruppy, Rett, Brent, Bart, Brady, Brandy & Buck, 1997

Carrol, "mama"

My seven sons have contributed to my role as the KING PIN QUEEN aboard, and when I look back, throughout history, realizing that all the great men of renown were only mamas' boys, I'm proud, too, seven-fold.

Mama's boys (left to right):
Ruppy, Rett, Brent, Bart, Brady & Brandy, 1996

Mamas' Boys

Tally up our mighty heroes.
Pin-point, one by one, each star,
and the times for them appointed
God-ordained for what they are.
Ah! to be so mad as Patton,
what redundant will to win,
paying dues to Rommel's genius,
yet, prepared to conquer him!
Champions win back pride and passion,
plucking lives from war and ruts.
Battles, aye, no pretty sight are
often won with blood and guts.
Oh! to run that race with Moshe
deeply burns endeavors still,
swift and sure commanding victory,
as the Six-Day-War reveals.
Warriors born in consecration,
driven onward, shouting fame;
forcing foes to second-guess them
just to beat them at their game.
So, while fervor fills the journals,
valor wraps each page like skin.
Ah, we, proud, beat breasts triumphant,
Mamas' boys made into men!

Wizened and frail now revived.
The decks of a soul scrubbed and swabbed.

Twilight, Dad on the back deck of our boat
in Hadlock, Washington

Created For You

Don't damage a heart that's touched heaven nor cast out someone who found love.
Take back, never, never, life given in pleasures few mortals dream of.
Uphold such a one safe with strong arms as inward revolts melt, subdued.
Now vanquished, surrendered without harm, one soul and one body for you.
Renewed while alone in your presence; sheer joy healing old inner wounds.
Elixir of virtues restore once, refreshed, resurrected from doom.
A world, cold, has offered temptations and danced on the backs of the weak,
but hinders the balm of redemption from creatures it throws to the deep.
The sea of despair changes faces as love lifts above and beyond.
One's walk on the water displaces one's weakness for that stronger bond.
Must shout it, this new found relation! Must sing it, heart surely will burst!
Assured with a brand new foundation; new love life for one once accursed.
So cherish the heart that's touched heaven, don't cast-out the one now in love.
No, never take back what's been given, this treasure few mortals know of.

In keeping with traditional song scribing, there's moonbeams for-sale for interested parties. Any party who has ever experienced his viewing from the deck of a ship, owns momentary moon-writes.

Texas moon, Gorman

Holding the Moon for Me

I never used to wonder 'bout the skies above,
or take the time to ponder nature's force and stuff.
But ever since we took each others hand in love,
I find myself at peace with things above.

Heaven holds the moon in place at sea, tonight,
and keeps the stars in space to guide each vessel right.
Won't let the sun ascend until the morning light,
and holds the moon for me, tonight.

It didn't matter much at all about the PLAN,
and not a lot of thought was sought on space's span.
But finding out Who keeps these works so well in hand,
I watch in admiration when I can.

Heaven holds the moon in place at sea, tonight,
and keeps the stars in space to guide each vessel right.
Won't let the sun ascend until the morning light,
and holds the moon for me, tonight.

In retrospect, there wasn't a home out of the three purchased, that worked for us during our early years of house-sitting. Either work fell-off, or circumstances beyond our control came about.

The roof we identified with, eventually, was mobile. Houses are like armor, a covering, a protection, but not for everyone.

Saddles are for horses but not for the rider who thinks with his pony, bareback.

San Jorge, Mexico

Priceless Pearl

Out on the edge where outcasts etch out niches hid from view,
With raiment made of different quirks and worn like passed-down shoes;
these, maverick, carve a slice of life that's spice and tucked inside;
their brand-less garb, each stitch portrays, still clad a weathered pride.
An oyster near the shoreline lies at home in rocky crag;
its shell exposed to seasons and disguised in nature's rags;
while inward soft flesh nurtures one fine jewel that's cultured, pure,
this rugged rock composure helps to keep its secret sure.
The balance on the edge has just two faces to protect,
be it mortal or immortal, there's honor both respect.
The gem each choose to steadfast watch, in this world or the next,
just anyone won't care to guard 'less they've one they'll invest.
Excitement and desire oft rise to share the prize discerned;
remoteness spreads her welcomed arms as crowds are unconcerned.
The outer-most will keep these badge-less drifters to itself.
Perhaps it's nature's lock and key for pearls of priceless wealth.

One evening standing on Lars and B.B.s' lanai, we watched as the moon started its path across the sky. As it slowly came closer awakening everything in its path below, we counted fruit trees, eatable plants, foliage (enormous, umbrella-like, monkey pod trees) on this beautiful piece of manicured land and anticipated the walk down the rocky path to sleep, to see if we were dreaming! Not only had they just built this house, but a bungalow built for two was awaiting us.

The Thanem Family: Rachael Leah, Gretchen Anne, B.B. (Mom), Joseph Walker (Joe), Trevor Morris (brat), Lars Alvin Jr. (Bo) & Lars (Dad).

B.B. on lanai looking to the sea...Hawaii

Harnessed Moon

The moon has cast its silver spell
upon the water's edge
and drawn this household's full atten-
-tion to the upstairs ledge.
Those ripples on the ocean only
'tend to taunt us more.
We watch from opened window waves
that shimmer towards the shore.
Ohia trees in silhouette seem
further than they are;
while cinder mixed with lava rocks
are home out in the dark.
Grey shadows hide as moonbeams stir
up hope on this lanai.
Thank God, we're in the tropics as
we view the yard outside!
Soon the moon will brighten up
the bungalow below
and spread its light on stony paths
which lead to our abode.
Each night we're always thankful as
the fragrance fills the room,
our little hut ideally built
to harness breeze and moon.

More thoughts on soul searching, humility and sizing up the place we are and belong, so we will be careful not to forget how we have needed a helping hand and shoulder, countless times!

Lonely roads....

The Journey

With each breath of life a journey's somewhere starting,
and the travel plan seems unclear for a while.
Though direction's shrouded often after parting,
common knowledge takes the lead for many miles.
Now and then a side track causes one to stumble;
from it, force him wander aimlessly for years.
If allowed, he'll back track to the road sign fumbled
and pickup the trail but, now, with added tears.
Know of some who think they've never lost their bearings
and walked straight and sure the stairway of ascent?
To one off the track these "some" pass by uncaring,
wrapped-up in self-ways, their helping hand is spent.
If your 'target's' set to trek across to heaven,
give some thought and render aid along the way.
One once left the "ninety-nine" to help a "has-been."
Maybe that was you or me who'd gone astray.
Don't let grudges crimp your style or destination.
Let forgiveness be allowed to rule your heart.
And remember brothers weakened from correction;
be the shoulder needed for another start!

This poem is in relation to the many storms we have weathered through the years, and summarizes the feelings of looking back at all the night-watches we were forced to stand.

Night Watchman

He watches from the wheel house far across the waters, blue,
passage long established since beginning's tide;
standing there to prove the cargo that was brought on by the crew
and their faithfulness to routines on the ride.
Though His vigil at the station doesn't hide the mates from woe
and their dread of squalls that blow along the shore.
Yet He'd walk across the water if was needed for their soul,
but, instead, withdraws to test their wits some more.
While the Ancient of all ancients from the cabin takes the wheel
as the storm tears through the rigging hard and long;
could this be a test of crewman's faith who claims that God is real
that He's walked the plank for every seaman's wrong?
Should this One in charge examine freight and find a load unsafe,
proving hazardous to boat and crew alike,
He'll demand unworthy burdens be committed to the waves
as He keeps the watch for them on through the night.

On one of our historic moves from Texas to Idaho, we had all our belongings divided in two pickups. Rup had the three boys and I the two girls. Somewhere in Jackson Hole, Wyoming we hit snow and it continued into the wee hours of the morning. This path was

unfamiliar to us, both, so kept on going, hoping there would be town just ahead. I'll never forget the feelings of forlorn with vision tunneled narrowly between the snow-piled banks and white-out. As despair would engulf, I would catch a faint light in the distance. Though only a ten-mile marker each time, it was enough to be my saving grace throughout the night.

Northwest night

Spark of Life

Where dwells the simple knowledge that was once regarded, dear,
now set aside like trash discarded, garbage to be, cleared?
Unholy works, unleashed, abound, nor less is left to learn,
as mankind licks its chops and woofs down arts that once were spurned.
This cunning form has raised its head to try both young and old,
instigating broken pledges, losing static clings control.
A form of ever learning, [illegible] coming doom,
the price tag for enlightenment and collected all too soon.
Somewhere the candle still burns low; flames, dim, have not waxed cold;
and wicks like faith not yet been snuffed, a source of warmth they hold.
These creatures know the terms they've met will make their conflict ease;
refusing to be faint of heart, their fight on earth's appeased.
Like fireflies midst the darkness glow to radiate they care,
these feeble, torch of energy, help rid lives from despair.
There's violence fraught with chaos and the homeland's bleak and dark.
It matters not how black the night, light gives life from one spark!

The sea is an unruly force; there men have lived, laughed, cried and died.

And there, man has made his peace with God.

La Pinta, Mexico
Bart & Lars

Pohoiko,
Hawaii

Sea Winds

Prevailing winds have been replaced as storms invade their course
arrayed in darkest shades of gray and over ride by force.
From up above the 'horsetails' fade as day's swept from the sky;
while 'gray beards' furl their frenzied caps, a mad sea's race to die!
A maelstrom for a boat this size, it sails, 'bone in her teeth.'
Each knot has quickened pace to meet opposing strength beneath.
Foreboding's felt from fearful dread. Death lingers near unseen.
No sign serene will rest content on board this driven fiend.
"Hull down," was last reported from a sighting early on.
Horizon swallowed up the craft and left this ship alone.
Despair and pain now grip and tear its inner chamber soul,
and nerves of steel have turned to clay as sickness heaves from roll.
Unyielding chance of rescue while this savage weather roars,
until sweet peace has been restored and SEA WINDS blow once more.

Kohala, Hawaii
(Maui in the background)

When hard times come we try to force ourselves to realize that no matter how tuff our situation, others have possibly had it worse.

Hopefully, this clears cob webs of forgetfulness and self-indulgence, so that we may render assistance in thought or deed.

Gleaning

Every where there's church bells ringing and a show of crowds respond.
Still the brothers in the by-ways and the highways loosen bonds.
And the synagogues of white wash seem to fill the sky with throngs
but neglect the courtyard's outcast mingled with the ones they've wronged.
In the tent within the circle shout great men with burning lamps.
Where's the few who've taken candles just for those left out in camp?
Labeled with these ones rejected let me too be one day named.
For with pretense they're accepted but in heart, mankind's ashamed.
So I pray the stand of Moses will be always clear to me,
to reject a "season's pleasure wrapped in wrong," and choose as he.
Fields are ripened for the harvest, naught but gleaning's to be done.
Children sneered the invitation; so the winning's for the bum.

While sharing the docks along the way, we've swapped dreams and visions, plus traded a few tall-tales with some God-only-knows-where-they're-headed ruffians and an occasional gentleman.

Some ideas were keepers, worth stowing; while others should have been flushed! The poem following is dedicated to Rup and the caretakers along the waterfront: a braided mix of outlaws with ideals.

Daydreaming...Rup on Texas farm, 1995

Rup on the balcony, San Jorge, Mexico

Don't Fence Him In

If every man had all dreams, one, and each approached one goal post
where one set rule would govern all by robots trained as cold hosts;
there'd been a lot of men extinct, who'd withered. Boredom's vic'try!
Just to exist, they ceased to live; their usefulness turned his'try.
Some still choose these who play their thoughts and dare to take some chances
by tossing out their bread to sea, returned in new romances.
Deliberate? These don't have time. That's only done in board rooms.
In new frontiers, perhaps on sea, they'll live and build, while dreams loom.
These push their thoughts on not one soul but share in private daydreams.
This in itself can keep alive these men built not for main streams.
Yes, you can say they're rebel born. Their bottom line's a good cause.
These fought in wars to win your rights. Will you cliche them 'outlaws'?
Permit them dreams. We'll gain in turn. These keep alive our senses.
We're much the richer if we don't put men like these in fences.

Almost as long as I have known Rup, he has worn bell bottoms. When they were removed from shelves because of fad, his remained. But the trouble finding them had us shaking bushes many times. Getting him out of those faded blues would be as impossible as erasing the sea from his soul. From our bungalow we listen to the surf break against the cliff and roll up on the beach at night. The silent thoughts that drift out into that night are quite familiar and easily interpreted...blues that won't fade!

Rup, 1995

Rup in the Navy, 1951

Tantalizing surf calling: "return to me..."

Faded Blues

He hears the surf as bedtime nears
and shadows start to drift.
Attentively, he listens as it
breaks against the cliff.
His health has let him know that he
should go back to the sea,
and so at night, in dreams, it seems
to say, "Return to me!"
There hasn't been a day gone by
since he was forced to shore,
that longing and desire have not
reminded him some more.
His life would never be the same
the day he first set sail;
nor could the knot it tied on this
old swabby ever fail.
And, "Once a sailor," so it goes,
with him it's never changed,
and matters not
a ship wreck knocked his 'sonar' out of range.
Tonight in silent thought his prayer,
again, is made anew.
As waves head out to sea, he's left
in faded bells of blue.

Same old saga of the man and the sea and his eagerness for the journey back to test the waters. Patience, ignored by my leader and his troops who've always had paint on their bottoms by evening from a skiff painted that morning.

Kona, Hawaii
Peggy, Davey & Pavy

Waipio Valley Big Island, Hawaii

Nanakuli Beach, Oahu, Hawaii, Kiawi tree

Without a Doubt

Without a doubt, if God allowed
a passage we could take,
we both, no doubt would go that route
before the morning break.
Of course it's plain that we'll remain
until it's right to go,
instructions clear on deafened ear
to places we don't know.
But still we scheme in made up dreams
for other friendly shores
and make believe we're almost free
to sail again once more.
We'll hold on here as we would there
with diligence and trust.
One day the 'wait' will make paths straight;
we'll be off as we must!
Somewhere an isle with kindly smiles
has placemats set for two;
a seaside beach within boat's reach
reserved for me and you.
We can't deny the ocean's tie,
what life on board's about.
And if God should, we really would
leave out without a doubt!

Rupert and Carrol, Alaska, 1985

Rup's not getting out that easy! He is forever pestering about the best poem being written when he checks out! That half way ticks me off! So, decided to write the last one, now, and then he won't be forced to bail out or change course.

Rup and Carrol today

Last Poem

If Rup were to leave me
alone in this world,
I'd lay down my pen, I'm
a right handed girl.
There'd be no more reason
to write of the past
with his future scribbled
in heaven at last!
My poems would be silent;
my prose then at rest;
for I with my sweetheart
had written our best.
His tale would be told.
I, with writer's block, cry.
I'm left without 'writes'
of my right handed guy.

Sea Journey in a Shell

Summing it all up: whether we tie knots at a Chapel in Las Vegas; or shake peanuts from a field in Central Texas; dodge dust devils in West Texas; fish the best streams in the Sawtooths of Idaho; eat oysters at the foot of the Olympics in Washington; watch the Golden Gate become obscure on the distant California shores; make the "catch of the day" out of Ketchikan, Alaska; wrap shrimp up in tortillas from Mexico's Sea of Cortez; travel the Alcan Highway through beautiful British Columbia, Canada; take one more sip of milk from a coconut on Hawaii's Big Island; life still remains for us just one long......

BOAT TRIP!

CAB

Carrol A. Buntin